■ AN INTRODUCTION TO ■

PHOTOGRAPHY

EDITED BY GAVIN HODGE

■ AN INTRODUCTION TO ■
PHOTOGRAPHY

MICHAEL FREEMAN
EDITED BY GAVIN HODGE

TIGER BOOKS INTERNATIONAL
LONDON

A QUINTET BOOK

This edition first published 1990 by
Tiger Books International PLC
London

Copyright © 1990 Quintet Publishing Limited
ISBN 1-85501-064-X

This book was designed and produced by
Quintet Publishing Limited
6 Blundell Street
London N7 9BH

Creative Director: Peter Bridgewater
Designer: Michael Morey
Project Editor: Gavin Hodge
Editor: Lindsay Porter

Typeset in Great Britain by
Central Southern Typesetters, Eastbourne
Manufactured in Hong Kong by
Regent Publishing Services Limited
Printed in Hong Kong by
Leefung-Asco Printers Limited

Some of the material in this publication
previously appeared in *How to Take and Develop
Black and White Photographs,* and *How to Take and
Develop Colour Photographs.*

CONTENTS

INTRODUCTION

BELOW Although advances in camera technology have taken much of the toil out of good photography, there is still no replacement for a good idea. In this instance, a fine silhouette against rich sunlight.

BELOW Although advances in camera technology have taken much of the toil out of good photography, there is still no replacement for a good idea. In this instance, a fine silhouette against rich sunlight.

OPPOSITE Black-and-white is undeniably the best choice for beginners, because the materials are so undemanding, yet its potential as a means of personal expression marks it as 'the craftsman's film'.

We live in a generation in which visual images are playing an increasingly important role, and understanding photography enables you to become visually articulate with comparative ease. Photography is a wonderful means of self-expression, and when the taking of photographs is allied to the making of photographs in the darkroom it leads to great fulfilment, and a logical climax to the sequence of events begun by seeing the picture in your mind's eye and pressing the shutter button.

Although we live in a coloured world the impact and graphic expression of black and white photography is considered by many to be superior to colour. Black-and-white reportage photographs in newspapers and magazines can, and regularly do, change our attitudes to the world around us. And in addition, one of the beauties of black-and-white is that it is an easy medium to control and manipulate in the darkroom.

Practically all photographers begin by shooting colour. It is initially convenient to let a laboratory turn your exposed film into prints, but if you have the makings of a photographer it is likely that you will quickly become dissatisfied with the poor quality and consistency, and small size of commercial prints. Many switch to transparencies which retain colour and detail better than any print. But if you wish you can also make your own colour enlargements in the darkroom, either from colour negative or transparency film.

This book is intended as an introduction to the basics of photography. It explains cameras, lenses and accessories, which are really just tools designed to help you express your thoughts in pictures, and it explains how to produce photographs from the original concept to the final image.

A taste of the wonderful diversity of the monochrome image. The image above, taken by an unknown photographer before the turn of the century, has been toned by the passing of time. John Thompson is responsible for the image (right) taken in China in the 1860s. The materials and equipment then available placed limitations on everyday, 'candid' photography. The scene is brilliantly posed. The remaining photograph (top right) illustrates how using natural light can preserve an authentic atmosphere.

OPPOSITE A thorough knowledge of the technical aspects of photography is vital in producing good colour work, however, when all is said and done, it is the human eye and brain that judge whether a particular scene is attractive and worthy of preserving on film.

1

CHOOSING EQUIPMENT

CAMERAS AND LENSES

Any modern camera, even an unsophisticated snapshot model, can be used for high-quality colour or black and white photography. Nevertheless, the simpler the camera, the more limitations it is likely to have, and it is important to know from the start just what your equipment is capable of. If, for instance, it has a single fixed lens, there will be types of photography that are beyond its scope – for example, anything that needs the high magnification of a telephoto lens, wide fields of view, or very close focusing.

This may, of course, be no disadvantage at all, particularly if you intend to concentrate on, say, candid photographs of people in everyday situations. If, on the other hand, you want to explore a variety of kinds of image and types of subject, a 'system' camera with interchangeable lenses (35mm single lens reflex) is the best choice.

As a guiding principle, tackle the areas of photography that your camera allows, or buy the equipment that your interests require. The 35mm SLR camera is by far the most common type used by people who have a serious interest in photography, so in this book the assumption is that this is the equipment you are using. Most of what is written still applies to snapshot cameras and larger formats, but if you have something other than a 35mm SLR, be prepared for slight differences here and there.

Finding the balance between technical proficiency and relying too much on equipment has always been one of the hidden difficulties facing photographers. The point of this balance varies from person to person, as some photographers are more comfortable when surrounded by a large selection of lenses and other items to cope with all contingencies, while others produce their best work when using the bare minimum. Whatever the case, there are two conflicting influences. Equipment alone does not produce pictures, but the sophistication and variety available in photographic stores is an obvious temptation, as well as being a source of pleasure in what is, after all, a technically-oriented activity. Believing that a new gadget automatically will improve the standard of your pictures, however, is over-optimistic. Equally, studied ignorance of photographic technique, with the idea that only an intuitive eye is needed, is just as misguided.

Here, we look at equipment as the tools necessary for the job. No more, no less. It may help, if you are still building up your range of equipment, or are planning to start, to think of two groups of items: basic equipment and, later, extras. A data-back, for example, may appeal as an ingenious toy, but it is unlikely to be a more important purchase than a first wide-angle lens. On the next few pages, we look at the way equipment selection can work in practice. Camera design changes constantly, partly as real improvement (making automatic metering produce more consistently reliable exposures, for instance) and partly as a way of encouraging photographers to spend more money. As the function of the camera body is fairly straightforward – to move the film along, control the exposure by means of a shutter, and measure what the exposure setting should be – there are few reasons for trading in old models for new every year. Most major manufacturers produce similar ranges; if you choose no more sophisticated a model than you really need, that will leave more money in the budget for lenses, which usually merit more attention.

If you have an SLR, its two most valuable properties are that you see exactly what will be exposed onto the film (through the viewfinder), and that you can use different lenses. A first priority, then, is to have a variety of lenses, for the focal length of the lens is what determines, to a large degree, the character of the picture. Standard focal lengths, which are around 50mm for a 35mm camera, give an angle of view and proportions that appear very much as the eye sees, and this is the lens that is usually sold with the camera.

Wide-angle lenses have shorter focal lengths, take in more of the scene and give a more pronounced perspective, making close objects seem larger in relation to those in the background. They

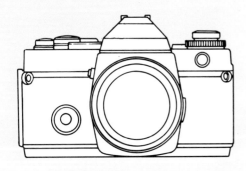

TOP RIGHT CANON EOS 750 QD Canon cameras have always been at the forefront of the electronic revolution. This model has built-in retractable flash allied to user-friendly controls.

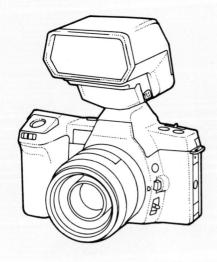

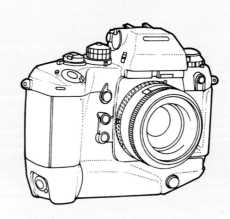

CENTRE RIGHT NIKON F4 A highly sophisticated autofocus 35mm SLR which is the heart of a huge system of lenses and accessories.

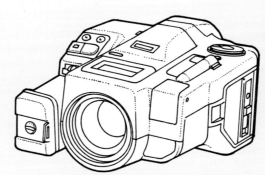

BOTTOM RIGHT RICOH MIRAI This futuristic design has a wide-ranging zoom lens built in, yet it is a single lens reflex (SLR) camera which lets you view the subject through the lens for accurate composition.

TOP LEFT OLYMPUS OM-4 Also a highly automated camera, the OM-4 is designed for near-foolproof operation in unskilled hands, but provides a highly sophisticated metering system for more experienced photographers.

CENTRE LEFT MINOLTA DYNAX 7000i Minolta pioneered efficient autofocus on 35mm SLRs. The Dynax 7000i has predictive autofocus for shooting moving subjects. It is shown fitted with an accessory flashgun – the MINOLTA PROGRAM 3200i.

BOTTOM LEFT LEICA M6 This 35mm rangefinder camera takes interchangeable lenses and is built to the highest standards. It rivals SLR cameras for versatility and image quality.

PENTAX 6x7 A 6x7cm medium format camera for professional use. Transparencies or negatives produced measure 6x7cm, giving excellent reproduction characteristics for commercial photography.

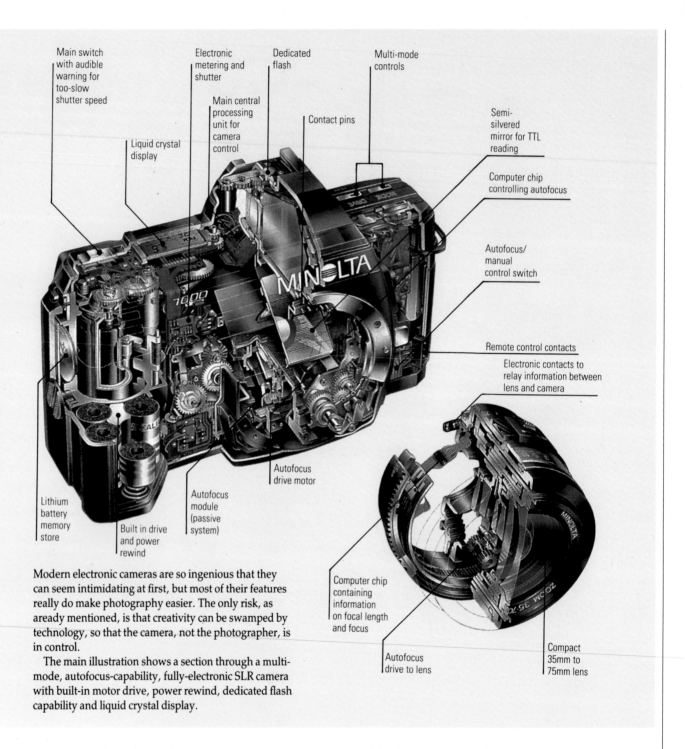

Main switch with audible warning for too-slow shutter speed

Electronic metering and shutter

Dedicated flash

Multi-mode controls

Liquid crystal display

Main central processing unit for camera control

Contact pins

Semi-silvered mirror for TTL reading

Computer chip controlling autofocus

Autofocus/ manual control switch

Remote control contacts

Electronic contacts to relay information between lens and camera

MINOLTA

7000

Lithium battery memory store

Built in drive and power rewind

Autofocus module (passive system)

Autofocus drive motor

Computer chip containing information on focal length and focus

Autofocus drive to lens

Compact 35mm to 75mm lens

Modern electronic cameras are so ingenious that they can seem intimidating at first, but most of their features really do make photography easier. The only risk, as aready mentioned, is that creativity can be swamped by technology, so that the camera, not the photographer, is in control.

The main illustration shows a section through a multi-mode, autofocus-capability, fully-electronic SLR camera with built-in motor drive, power rewind, dedicated flash capability and liquid crystal display.

can be used to draw the viewer into the scene and feel some sense of immediacy and involvement. At the other end of the scale, telephoto lenses have long focal lengths, magnifying the view of distant subjects, and giving a flattening effect on perspective. Mirror lenses employ a different principle to arrive at a similar effect, with a combination of lens and mirror, similar to that used in some telescopes, to achieve high magnification. Zoom lenses cover a variety of focal lengths continuously by means of

a larger number of individual glass elements which move inside the lens barrel. Different models cover different ranges.

A basic selection of lenses for many people, particularly those starting in photography, would normally be a single SLR body with either three lenses of fixed focal length or one or two zoom lenses to cover a similar range. The fixed focal length lenses would be one standard, one moderate wide-angle, and one moderate telephoto. Zoom lenses

ABOVE A 28mm wide-angle lens can lend drama to a landscape scene. Depth of field is great, and even focusing becomes a secondary consideration.

LENS EFFECTS

A good demonstration of the characteristics of lenses is to choose a single scene and shoot it using lenses of different focal lengths, ranging from very short to very long. This exercise can aid your awareness of the compositional possibilities offered by each lens.

ABOVE Very much the 'standard' wide-angle, a 35mm lens still retains the characteristic of increasing the apparent distance between subjects common to lenses with short focal lengths.

ABOVE A 50mm standard lens approximates the angle of view as seen by the human eye.

ABOVE One of the moderate telephotos, a 135mm lens enables the photographer to enlarge the subject within the frame from a distant viewpoint.

LEFT Producing good subject magnification, a 200mm lens offers a relatively small depth of field, making focusing critical.

have the advantage of combining the variety of focal length in a single piece of equipment, and make for a lighter load to carry around. Their disadvantages are that they are usually individually heavier than comparable fixed focal length lenses, and that the maximum aperture is smaller. (Smaller apertures mean slower shutter speeds, and make low-light photography less easy.)

Lenses vary in the quality of their manufacture and the maximum aperture (often referred to as the 'speed' of a lens: f/1.4 is fast for a standard lens, f/2.8 quite slow). Still, the most important difference is the focal length. Think in terms of what would be the ideal range for you and your preferred subjects. The more extreme the focal length on either side of the standard 50mm, the more exaggerated the effect on the image, and the more expensive the lens. Personal taste is the only

guide to follow, but the high sales of wide-angle lenses of around 28mm focal length, and of telephoto lenses around 135mm, show what the majority of people tend to choose.

Apart from focal length, other important distinctions among lenses involve special uses. Most of these, by definition, fall outside the category of basic equipment, but one is sufficiently popular to consider here. A macro lens has the ability to focus closely and give magnified views of small subjects, generally up to half life-size (normal lenses do not focus down so closely, giving a maximum enlargement of around one-seventh life-size). The optical quality of a macro lens at these close-focusing distances is, of course, high, but as this kind of lens also does a good job at normal distances, many photographers make it double up as their standard lens. Many zoom lenses have a 'macro' facility.

ANGLES OF VIEW

Compare the 62° angle of view of a 35mm wide-angle (1) with the 46° of a 55mm standard lens (2) and the even narrower view offered by a 180mm telephoto (3).

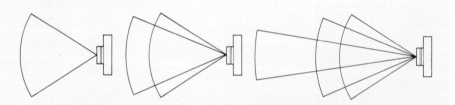

WIDE-ANGLE LENS

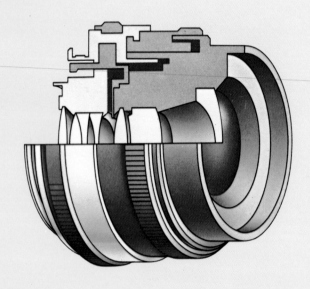

Wide-angle lens The 24mm lens (left) with an angle of view of 84 degrees, uses a retrofocus design to lengthen its extremely short focus so that it can be used with the reflex mirror in the camera housing. To overcome the problem of poor image quality at close focusing, the elements 'float' inside the housing. Their relative positions can therefore be changed as the lens focuses closer. In use, depth of field is relatively large while perspective is greatly exaggerated.

STANDARD LENS

Standard lens This 50mm standard lens presents the world approximately as the human eye sees it, giving a 46 degree angle of view that gives a 'natural' perspective and a moderately wide minimum aperture of f2 (although f1.8 maximum aperture are by far the most common on today's 50mm standards). Its six elements in four groups allow the manufacturer design flexibility to correct most common aberrations. In use (above right) the lens proves an ideal all-rounder, with its relatively fast maximum aperture allowing the photographer to work in low-light conditions.

LONG-FOCUS LENS

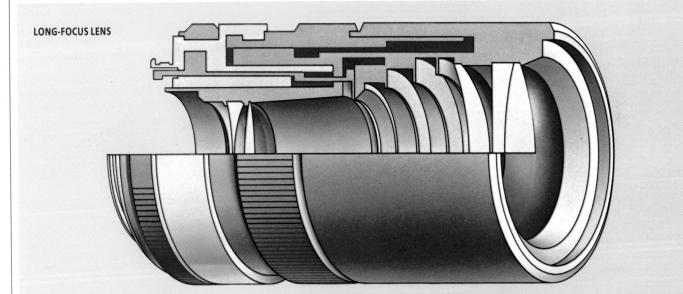

Long-focus lens A favourite among many photo-journalists, this fast 180mm telephoto lens has a maximum aperture of f2.8, which makes it fairly easy to hand-hold at quite slow speeds. For colour work in poor lighting conditions it is an ideal telephoto. Many lenses of this focal length tend to be heavy for their size, but this can be an advantage, as they lie steady in the hand. In use (right) perspective is compressed while focusing can be quite critical.

ACCESSORIES AND SUPPORTS

Accessories cover the range of extra equipment beyond the simple combination of camera and lens. What is considered a necessary extra is, however, largely a matter of opinion. Some filters are a useful addition, but the most effective are those that do a basic job of altering the colour values and tonal qualities, rather than achieving the trick effects that receive the most publicity in photography magazines. A basic set includes some light balancing filters, colour correction filters for common lighting problems (such as fluorescent illumination), a polarizing filter, colourless ultraviolet and a neutral (grey) graduated filter.

A shoulder bag is the usual way of carrying cameras, lenses, film and various odds and ends. Simple is better than fancy, because bags that advertise you as a photographer do nothing to help the picture and could potentially make candid photography more difficult. Choose a bag just large enough for what you need, that is, for shooting and carrying around. A large, multi-pocketed case is only useful if you have the equipment to fill it, and even then you may not find it much of a pleasure to carry around for long.

One last item of basic equipment, even if you do not carry it with you constantly, is a tripod. Bulky and awkward though it may be, it is the best answer for situations that call for slow shutter speeds. A room interior shot with good depth of field, an evening landscape, city lights at night, or a close-up are examples of types of picture in which hand-holding will not normally do the job. Even in good light, a tripod is a powerful aid to composition, making it easier to align things exactly in the viewfinder, and, of course, add a cable release.

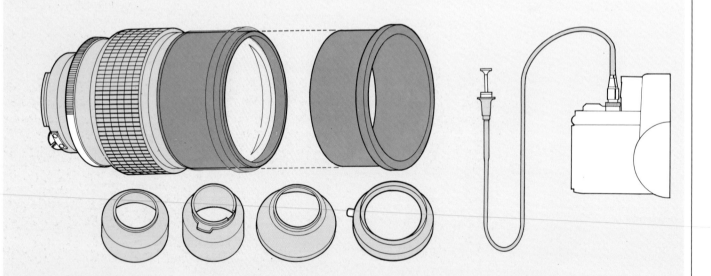

Lens hoods are designed to prevent flare by stopping stray rays of light from reaching the front element of the lens. As the illustration here shows, the hoods come in various shapes and lengths to suit the various focal lengths; a long hood on a wide-angle lens would result in a blacking out of a large section of the image, while a short, flared hood on a telephoto lens would not do its job at all. Although add-on hoods that screw onto the front of lenses are still widely available, built-in hoods designed for particular focal lengths are becoming ever-more common. Add-on hoods are available both in plastic and in soft rubber or a similar material, which collapses to facilitate ease of carrying.

ABOVE Cable releases are an important way of reducing vibration. They come in varying lengths and can be locked during long exposures.

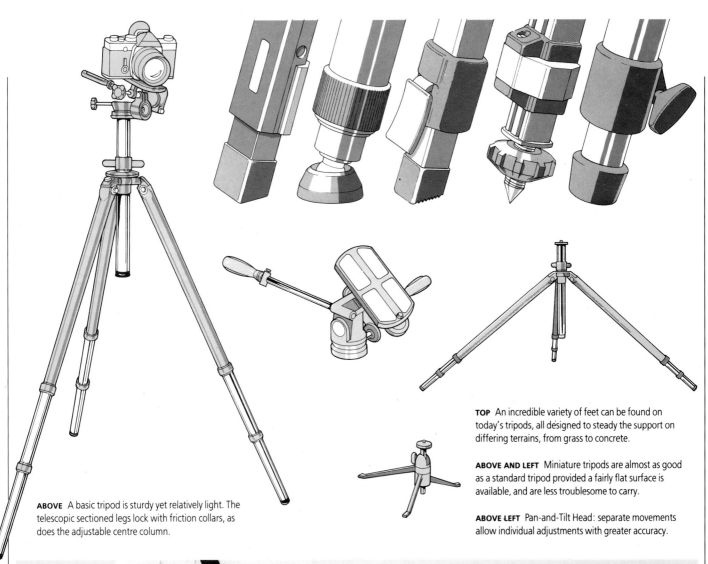

TOP An incredible variety of feet can be found on today's tripods, all designed to steady the support on differing terrains, from grass to concrete.

ABOVE AND LEFT Miniature tripods are almost as good as a standard tripod provided a fairly flat surface is available, and are less troublesome to carry.

ABOVE LEFT Pan-and-Tilt Head: separate movements allow individual adjustments with greater accuracy.

ABOVE A basic tripod is sturdy yet relatively light. The telescopic sectioned legs lock with friction collars, as does the adjustable centre column.

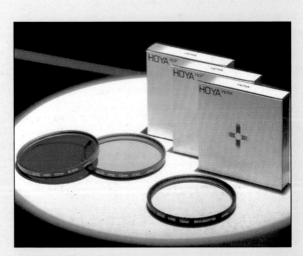

ABOVE A basic set of filters can include colour-correction neutral, graduated, polarizing, and light balancing filters.

LEFT A wide range of soft camera bags are available, many with an array of pockets to carry such items as film and filters, plus purpose-built pouches to hold zooms and fixed focal-length lenses.

EQUIPPING A DARK ROOM

PROCESSING EQUIPMENT

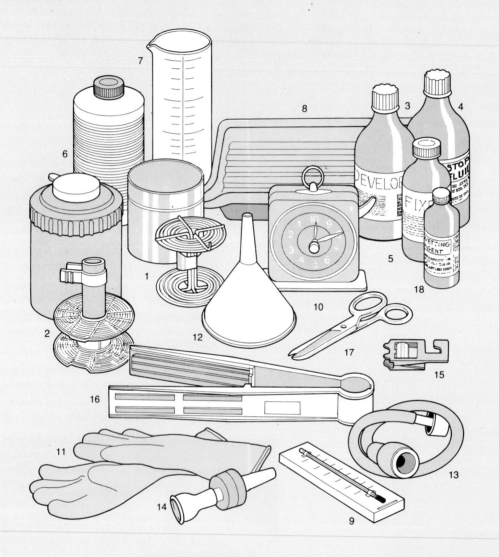

Developing tanks are available in two basic designs – with a stainless steel reel (1), and with a plastic reel (2) which is easier to load but less durable. Developer (3), stop bath (4), and fixer (5) should be kept in clearly-labelled, light-tight stoppered bottles; an even better alternative is an expanding container with a concertina shape (6) which adjusts so that air is excluded. For mixing chemicals, a graduated measuring flask (7) is essential, and to maintain them at a constant 68°F (20°C) they should be placed in a tray (8) filled with water at that temperature using a thermometer (9). A timer (10) can be pre-set to the recommended developing and fixing times. Rubber gloves (11) prevent skin irritation from prolonged contact with the chemicals and a funnel (12) prevents spillage when returning chemicals to the bottles. A water hose (13) and filter (14) are used for washing the film, which is then hung to dry on clips (15). Excess moisture can be removed with a pair of squeegee tongs (16). The film is finally cut into strips with scissors (17). Wetting agent (18) is added to the final wash to help the developer spread more easily and to prevent drying marks.

THE BLACK-AND-WHITE DARKROOM

One of the great pleasures in black-and-white photography is being able to follow through the entire process of making an image, from the moment of shooting to the finished print. Arguably, this applies even more to black-and-white than to colour, as the image is more susceptible to control and manipulation. Black-and-white photographers become used to anticipating the darkroom processes even when they are making the exposure: as we will see later in this book, knowing what changes can be made during processing and printing makes it possible to choose exposure settings accordingly.

The immediate stage once a roll of film has been exposed is to develop and fix it, and the equipment and chemicals needed are extremely simple.

Both 35mm and rollfilm are normally processed in a small circular tank, which is made either of stainless steel or plastic. These are available in different heights, depending on whether one or several films are to be processed at the same time, and the film itself is wound onto a spiral reel. Stainless steel reels load from the inside outwards, whereas plastic reels are grooved for the film to slide inwards, starting at the edge. The lid contains a hole fitted with a light baffle, so that processing solutions can be poured in and out without exposing the film to light. Once loaded, the tank can be used in normal lighting.

Darkness is, however, essential for taking the film out of its cassette and loading it into the tank. The darkroom that you use for printing can double for film loading, but the light-proofing is then even more critical. If you do not have the luxury of a room that can be given over full-time to darkroom use, it is not too difficult to make a temporary conversion of some other room. This is easiest if there is no window, but if there is, it can be blocked out either with a special type of roller blind, or with a solid shutter. A darkroom roller blind fitting is constructed as a box covering the window frame, in which a thick black cloth blind runs inside recessed grooves. The door is another potential source of light: cover the gaps with either draught-excluding flaps or foam strips.

Finally, check the effectiveness of the light-proofing. This can be done by taking out a short strip of unexposed film, covering part of it with an opaque object, and exposing it in the darkened room for a minute or two. Process it and see if you can distinguish the edge of the object that was covering it; if there is a noticeable demarcation of tone, the film has been fogged slightly and the room's light-proofing is not total.

An alternative to a darkroom is a changing bag, which is a double-lined bag of black material fitted with two zips and elasticated sleeves for your arms. Choose one that is large enough to work in easily.

The other equipment you will need is: a bottle opener to open the 35mm film cassettes, scissors to trim the ends, one or two graduates for measuring the mixing solutions (they should be at least as big as the developing tank), storage bottles, thermometer and stirring paddle. Temperature control is by no means as critical as it is for colour film development, but you will need a source of warm water and a fairly deep tray in which to stand the developer. Clips for hanging the washed film and a clean, dry place in which to hang them complete the list of essentials.

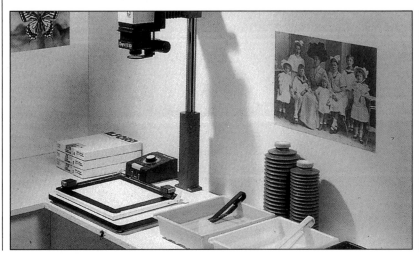

LEFT Standard set-up for black-and-white enlargement.

19

A MAKESHIFT DARKROOM

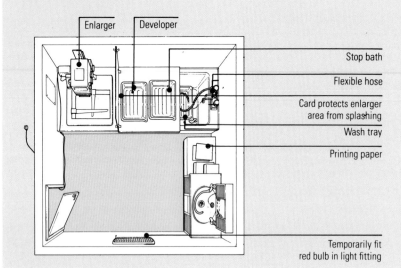

Enlarger

Developer

Stop bath

Flexible hose

Card protects enlarger area from splashing

Wash tray

Printing paper

Temporarily fit red bulb in light fitting

A bathroom has certain advantages for temporary conversion: plumbing, large water containers, and disposal. In the conversion above, a board over most of the bath provides a working surface. Print washing takes place underneath, in the bath itself. Power for the enlarger should be taken from outside the bathroom, for safety reasons.

A CONVERTED STUDY

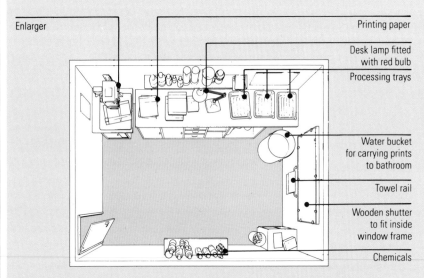

Enlarger

Printing paper

Desk lamp fitted with red bulb

Processing trays

Water bucket for carrying prints to bathroom

Towel rail

Wooden shutter to fit inside window frame

Chemicals

A slightly more sophisticated type of conversion, yet still temporary, is of an office or study. Even if there is no plumbing, processing solutions can be mixed and brought in from the bathroom, while a plastic bucket can be used for taking fixed prints out for washing. The room can be light-proofed with a wooden shutter that fits tightly into the window frame, and felt or rubber flaps around the door.

■ ENLARGER & PRINTING EQUIPMENT

Unlike colour, black-and-white photography is geared totally towards printing. With the very minor exception of slides for projection (Agfa make a reversal film, and Polaroid 35mm instant films give a positive image), black-and-white films are only a preliminary stage. The end-product that justifies the effort is an enlarged print. After the camera equipment, the most important item is an enlarger.

Fortunately, a black-and-white enlarger is neither as complex nor as expensive as an enlarger designed for colour printing. There is no need for colour filters (either a red safety filter fitted to some models

for swinging in front of the lens, and the filter set used with variable-contrast paper), and the colour balance of the lamp is not so important.

Nevertheless, a good enlarger is a significant investment, and ought to be chosen carefully. First, the size: enlargers are available for all film formats up to sheet film, and the larger sizes will accept all smaller formats. If you think that you might up-grade from 35mm to rollfilm at some point, it is worth getting a medium-format enlarger to begin with. Two focal lengths of enlarger lens will then allow you to print both sizes of negative. As with the camera, what ultimately decides the image

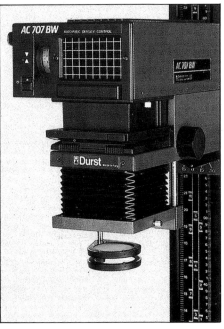

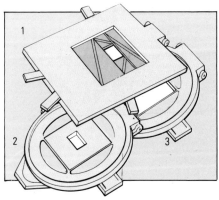

BELOW Film carrier types include an adjustable mask for different film formats (**1**), a glass carrier to hold thin film flat (**2**), and a hinged plate (**3**).

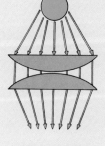

ABOVE There are two basic choices when deciding upon an enlarger head for black-and-white printing; one that features a diffuser lamp, which spreads the light over a large area and is more forgiving, or one which has a condenser lamp, where the light is focused from the small lamp on the negative.

quality is the quality of the lens. This is no place to skimp; the enlarger lens should be at least as good as your camera lenses, otherwise you will have wasted their value. For normal enlargements, use a lens that has the same focal length as the standard lens for the format. 50mm or 60mm are the usual choice for 35mm, 80mm or 90mm for rollfilm.

The head of the enlarger contains the light source, and there are two alternative systems: condensers or diffused lamps. In the first, condenser lenses, usually different for each focal length of enlarging lens, focus the light from a small lamp on the negative; in the second, the light is from a large area, and is unfocused and diffuse. Condensers give a slightly sharper image on the print, although they also make the film grain and any blemishes appear more prominently.

An easel is needed to hold the paper in place and give a neat border to the image. The normal design has adjustable masks – strips of metal or plastic – that can be altered for different proportions and sizes. A focusing magnifier focuses on the grain of the negative, and is useful for getting the sharpest possible images.

Contact prints, which are normally made as a means of selecting photographs, are made by pressing the negative strips against a sheet of printing paper. A sheet of plain glass will do, but a purpose-built contact printing frame is easier to use.

Other equipment includes a safelight, anti-static brush for cleaning negatives, dodging tools, and processing trays with tongs (if you use different sizes of paper, different sets of trays make more economical use of the processing solutions).

ENLARGER LIGHT SOURCES

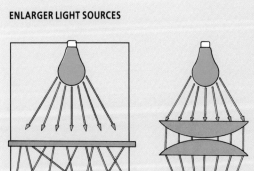

DIFFUSER SYSTEM   CONDENSER SYSTEM

The two alternative systems are diffusion and condenser, and each produces a distinctive quality of image. In a diffusion head, the light source is made even by a translucent screen; in the condenser system, two lenses focus the beam. Diffusers are normally preferred for colour.

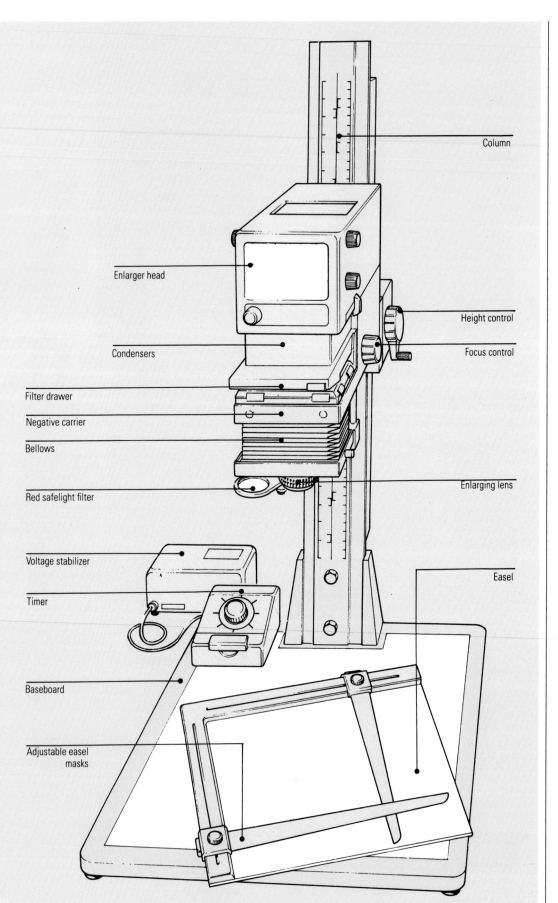

MAINTENANCE CHECKLIST

Check for the following faults:

1 Dirt on the lens. Causes flare and vague dark spots when stopped down.

2 Dirt on condensers or filters. Causes soft-edged dark spots on print at small apertures.

3 Wrong condensers. Make sure they match the focal length of the enlarging lens.

4 Unsteady baseboard. Causes double or blurred image.

5 Torn bellows or gaps in enlarger head. Can cause fogging of print.

6 Condensers badly adjusted. Causes darkening towards edges of projected image.

7 Wrong enlarging lens. If lens does not cover negative, illumination and image quality fall off toward the edges of the projected image.

8 Focus gears slip. Causes soft focus. Tighten locking screws or relubricate.

RIGHT Black-and-white enlargers tend to be more simple than their colour counterparts, offering a basic means of exposing an image on a negative to light-sensitive paper.

Column

Enlarger head

Height control

Focus control

Condensers

Filter drawer

Negative carrier

Bellows

Enlarging lens

Red safelight filter

Voltage stabilizer

Easel

Timer

Baseboard

Adjustable easel masks

THE COLOUR DARKROOM

Now that colour film development has been largely standardized to two simple processes, very little darkroom equipment is needed to process your own rolls. With few exceptions, most colour films can be developed by Kodak's E-6 process (for slides) or C-41 process (for colour negatives). Processes with different names from other manufacturers, such as Fuji, are basically look-alikes, and the differences are minor. The main exception is Kodachrome slide film which has its own process. The E-6 process requires 11 steps and 7 solutions; the C-41 family uses 7 steps and 4 solutions. These stages determine the number of containers that you will need for mixing and storing.

The basic unit for processing film is a spiral reel tank. The tank consists of a spiral reel, onto which the film is wound, and a container with a tight-fitting lid. The lid has a central hole with a light-proof baffle for the adding and pouring out of solutions, and there is usually a small cap fitted so that the entire tank can be inverted during processing. The sturdiest tanks are made of stainless steel, and many people find this type of reel the easiest to load. An alternative is a plastic tank, with a grooved reel that is loaded by sliding the film in from the edge towards the centre.

For removing the film from its cassette and loading it into the spiral-reel tank, absolute darkness is essential. The most comfortable space in which to work is a purpose-built darkroom, or at least an understairs cupboard, bathroom or utility room that can be light-proofed for occasional use. Shutters or black cloth blinds that run in deep recesses are the usual ways of dealing with windows, although it is easier to start with a windowless area, if you have one. Doors can be light-proofed either with rubber draught-excluding strips, or with foam strips fitted into the frame. To check the effectiveness of the light-proofing, stay inside with the door closed for about 20 minutes, until your eyes have become accustomed to the dark. If you can see no chinks of light anywhere, and cannot see your hand if you move it in front of your face, the darkness is probably sufficient. As a final check, take a short un-exposed strip of fast colour film (pull this from the end of a fresh 35mm cassette), and lay it out in the darkness with something solid covering a part of it. Leave it there for about a minute, and then process it. When it has been washed and dried, examine it carefully for any signs of fogging; if there is any, it will be most obvious at the edge of the object that was on top of it.

If a darkroom is impractical, film can still be loaded and unloaded in a changing bag.

Other processing equipment includes graduates, clearly marked with centilitres or cubic centimetres (metric measurements have taken over almost totally from pints and fluid ounces), a thermometer, a stirring paddle to mix solutions, bottles for storing the solutions, and an effective means of maintaining the right temperature. Various brands of dish warmer are available, but a home-made alternative is a warm-water bath.

ENLARGER AND PRINTING EQUIPMENT

The simplest and cheapest enlarger that you can use for colour is, in fact, a plain black-and-white model, using its filter drawer with a set of colour printing filters (which are usually made of acetate). Make sure that the filters are the same size as the drawer; 3in (75mm) is standard. Also make sure that the enlarger is equipped with a focal length of lens that suits the film format you use: 35mm film, for example, needs an enlarger lens of 50mm or 60mm; 120 rollfilm should have an 80mm lens. Easier to use, but also more expensive, is a colour-head enlarger. The light source for this is designed for accurate colour reproduction, and the necessary filtration is built into the head. The usual system is a set of three dials or knobs, each of which turns a dichroic filter. These filters, one yellow, one magenta and one cyan (blue-green), can be dialled to different strengths. If the area where you live is subject to voltage fluctuations, a voltage regulator is useful too; otherwise, a voltage drop will affect not only the exposure (which is not too important) but also the colour balance.

RIGHT Some tanks, like the 1500 system from Jobo, accept two different reels; in this case their 1501 reel for 35mm, 120 and 220 film, and the 1502 reel for 110.

23

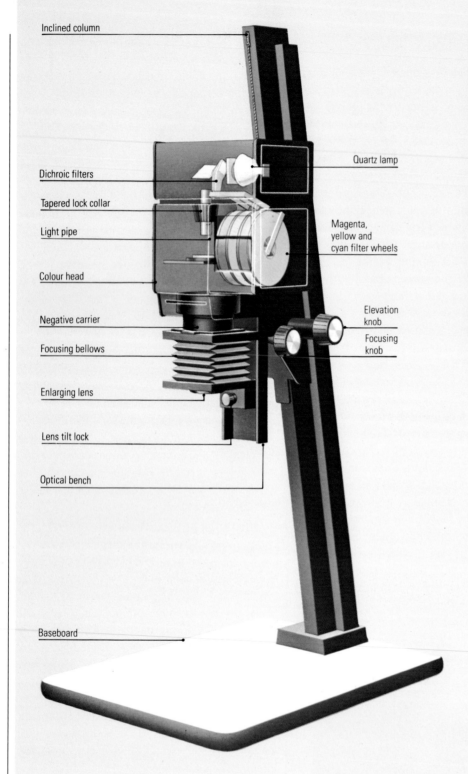

Inclined column

Dichroic filters

Tapered lock collar

Light pipe

Colour head

Negative carrier

Focusing bellows

Enlarging lens

Lens tilt lock

Optical bench

Baseboard

Quartz lamp

Magenta,
yellow and
cyan filter wheels

Elevation
knob

Focusing
knob

ENLARGER WITH COLOUR HEAD

This advanced enlarger, fitted with a colour head, uses a standard quartz halogen lamp as its light source, but transmits the light through an acrylic light pipe that absorbs the ultra-violet radiation that would upset colour balance in printing. For focusing accuracy, the enlarger's fine controls are mounted on a vertical optical bench which itself is attached to the main column. The degree of enlargement is controlled by moving the whole assembly up or down on the column: the image is then focused with the bellows.

For colour printing, three dials are mechanically linked to three filters (below) which can be placed partially or completely in the path of the light from the quartz lamp. The amount that each filter interrupts this light path determines the filtration. Less expensive enlargers use a filter drawer above the negative camera; different strengths of gelatin filters can then be inserted by hand.

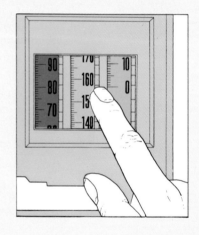

On the enlarger's baseboard you will need an easel for mounting the paper. This has a means of locating the paper and adjustable masks to crop the image to the exact size and shape that you want. Focusing can often be done well enough by eye alone, but a focusing magnifier allows you to focus precisely on the grain of the film.

Other things that you will need are an enlarger timer (it is much more convenient to have this connected to the enlarger's power supply than to operate a switch yourself), a blower brush for cleaning negatives, 'dodging' tools, and a safelight, the actual filter for which depends on the type of paper you use.

2

CHOOSING FILM

BLACK-AND-WHITE OR COLOUR?

Although the vast majority of photographers begin by shooting colour, the elemental appeal of black-and-white photography, coupled with the relative simplicity of home processing black-and-white wins many converts to the medium. Also, if you hope to earn cash with your camera there are countless newspapers and magazines crying out for good quality black-and-white illustrations.

There is also a ready market for colour in magazines, and for this you will need to provide transparencies, not colour prints. If you shoot a great deal of colour transparencies you could consider lodging the very best of them with a picture library. Picture libraries supply images to advertisers and publishers and constantly need to update their stock. It is a highly competitive field and you would do well to see what type of pictures are good sellers rather than expect a library to take your personal favourites.

Colour print film is ideal for personal photography – making a year by year record of your family and friends, and recording holidays. Colour print film is also a popular medium for club photographers who like to exhibit prints in club competitions. It is also worth noting that if you have a black-and-white darkroom you can easily make black-and-white prints from colour negatives if you wish, although tonal rendition will not be quite so accurate as it is with panchromatic black-and-white film.

MOUNTING AND LABELLING TRANSPARENCIES

Make sure, above all, that transparencies are adequately protected and properly identified. Develop a system for logging in transparencies, stamping your name, copyright mark, date and description on them. If a publisher uses a transparency for reproduction – many amateur photographers are now finding outlets for their work – it will have to be removed from the mount, so be prepared to re-mount used transparencies.

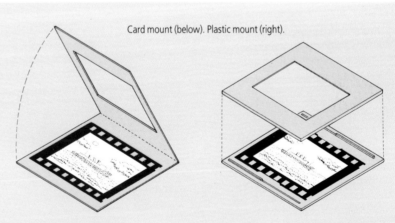

Card mount (below). Plastic mount (right).

© Michael Freeman 1978

INTERIOR OF MUSEO DE BELLAS ARTES, MEXICO CITY

Mexico 21 2695

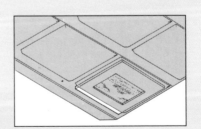

ABOVE A convenient filing system is to use transparent sheets, each containing individual pouches. These will fit into a standard filing cabinet.

A red spot in the lower left-hand corner of the mount (below) facilitates assembly for projection. To signify a sequence, rule a diagonal line (right) across the edges.

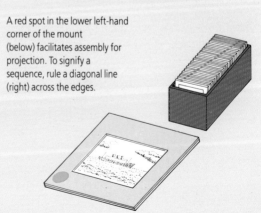

SLIDE OR PRINT?

In making some sense of the enormous variety of colour films available – there are many different types from different manufacturers – the first step is to settle on an end-product. Although it is possible to shoot both prints and slides (alternating, perhaps, or having a second camera body to allow an on-the-spot choice) most people tend to stick with one or the other.

If you are undecided, consider the pros and cons of each. A print is the natural way of looking at any picture – it can be seen in normal lighting conditions, and is tangible. It can be mounted, framed, hung on a wall, or placed in an album. Getting faithful colour reproduction and a full range of tones, however, takes time and skill (this, on the other hand, is part of the attraction of colour printing for many people).

One of the great advantages of slides is that, being projected by a bright light source, they appear to have considerable 'punch' – brighter highlights and a more immediate visual impact than a print. The process of photography with slide film is also simpler. As soon as it is processed, the film is ready for viewing. On the down-side, slides are not so convenient to look at. For their best effect, they need certain viewing conditions: principally, dark surroundings and a good, purpose-built screen. A slide show often has the nature of a performance, a disadvantage for some, but lending a sense of occasion to the images.

There are two standard designs of 35mm slide projector, the revolving drum type magazine (such as this Kodak Carousel) (left), and the sliding tray type (below).

26

TRANSPARENCY OR NEGATIVE

Having decided whether prints or slides will be the final form of your photography, this does not automatically determine the kind of film you should buy. Prints can be made from either negatives or transparencies, and the different processes ensure that the resulting images have different qualities. To contrast just two examples, the visual character of prints from negatives and of Cibachrome prints made directly from transparencies are highly distinctive, and immediately recognizable to any photographer who has some experience of colour printing. Side-by-side, there is little doubt that prints from negatives have a more subtle range of tones, a broader scale of contrast, and they allow the printer more control.

Nevertheless, delicate, controlled images do not always serve the needs of photographers, and the snappy colour intensity of Cibachrome, Ektachrome

PRINTS FROM SLIDES

Prints made from slides on Cibachrome, Ektachrome RC or other such papers are noted for their richness of colour. Even slides that lack contrast and punch can benefit from this treatment. While some colour reversal papers are like negative papers, as their colours are formed during development, others are dye destruction papers (Cibachrome) in which already present dyes are destroyed during the processing in proportion to the projected image.

RC, or similar processes may well suit the image much better. Subjects and images with rich colours and dramatic compositions often do very well printed by a positive/positive process from a slide, and images that lack sufficient contrast for your taste will also benefit. If you have slides and prefer to use a negative printing process, one alternative is to have 'internegatives' made. These are copies of a transparency onto a special colour negative emulsion that is designed to keep the contrasts low (copying and duplicating on ordinary film tends to increase contrast). Unless you have experience of making internegatives, it is best to give these to a laboratory to do.

Finally, it is possible to convert negatives into slides for projection, by copying them onto a special emulsion, such as Kodak Vericolor Slide Film. Again, this is a process that is best left to a professional laboratory, and is used only occasionally.

PRINTS FROM INTERNEGATIVES

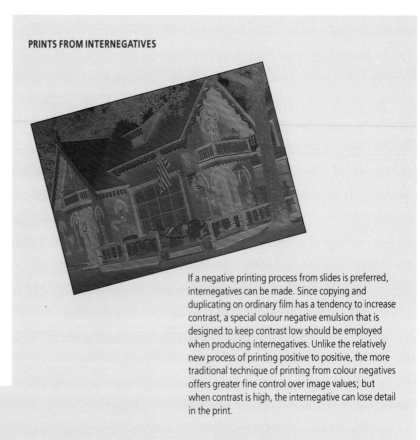

If a negative printing process from slides is preferred, internegatives can be made. Since copying and duplicating on ordinary film has a tendency to increase contrast, a special colour negative emulsion that is designed to keep contrast low should be employed when producing internegatives. Unlike the relatively new process of printing positive to positive, the more traditional technique of printing from colour negatives offers greater fine control over image values; but when contrast is high, the internegative can lose detail in the print.

FILM SPEED – SLOW OR FAST?

A black-and-white negative can vary in only a few ways. The most obvious is in how dark or light it is overall, and this is simply a matter of how much exposure the film is given in the camera and how much development in the darkroom. The more of each the film receives, the more of the emulsion will be darkened.

Three other qualities, however, are closely related to the way the film is made. They are speed, graininess and contrast. We will look at each of these in turn in a moment, but it is important to realize that they are all intimately related. The conventional way of making a film more sensitive to light is for the manufacturer to use bigger crystals of silver halide and to stack them in a thicker layer. This means that, when exposed and developed, the black silver grains form bigger clumps, and this becomes visible as a more grainy texture. You cannot have fast speed without some increase in graininess. Equally, contrast is related to speed in that slow films have a notably higher contrast than fast emulsions.

As we have just seen, choosing a black-and-white film means deciding on priorities, and the principal choice is between film speed and graininess. Were it possible to discount the effects of grain, there would be no need for different film speeds. As it is, there is a range, the fastest being several times more light-sensitive than the slowest.

Film speed depends mainly on the size and shape of the crystals in the emulsion. A large crystal exposed to the same amount of light as a small crystal can be developed just as easily to black silver, and is more visible because of its size. Also, if the grains are flat rather than lumpy, as in some of the latest films, and if these grains are aligned so that the flat side faces the light, they will react more readily. The amount of development and the chemistry of the developer can also be used to make film behave as if it were faster.

In practice, the sensitivity of film is referred to in terms of its speed. An average emulsion – medium-speed, in other words – is one that allows the camera to be used conveniently in most natural lighting. This means a shutter speed of around 1/125sec and an aperture setting somewhere in the middle of the range on the lens. This is a fairly vague definition, and in order to be able to calibrate the camera controls and make accurate exposures, film speed has a standard scale to which all makes now conform. The universally accepted measurement is the ISO number. ISO stands for International Standards Organisation, and the rating is made up of two numbers. The first is the equivalent of the old ASA figure, the second is equivalent to the system used mainly in Germany: DIN.

A medium-speed film has an ISO rating of between 100/21° and 125/22°. In normal practice, the second figure means so little outside Germany that it is normally dropped.

Film speeds have become standardized over the years, and there are now just three main categories: slow, medium and fast. Slow films are between ISO25 and 32, medium between ISO100 and 125 and fast at ISO400. In addition there are some specialized black-and-white emulsions with more extreme ratings – for instance, high-contrast lith films rated at around ISO12 and surveillance films rated over ISO1000.

A fast film is more convenient to use in practically every way than a slow film. It can be used in poorer light, allows a faster shutter speed (and so less chance of a blurred image through camera shake) and a smaller aperture (for better depth of field). The only circumstances in which this might not be wanted are if you need a slow shutter speed with shallow depth of field. Nevertheless, choosing the film speed involves other factors, notably graininess, which we deal with in detail next.

BELOW As a general rule, slower films display richer, more vibrant colours than their faster counterparts, and will always give sharper results.

LEFT Because black-and-white films that are more sensitive to light use bigger crystals of silver halide stacked in thick layers, fast emulsions feature very noticeable grain. On the other hand, using slow films (as in this example) results in very fine grain and, therefore, higher contrast.

RIGHT While an increase in grain is an unavoidable consequence of using fast films, the photographer who produces small prints may not find the trait a problem.

BELOW With faster films the larger the print the more noticeable the grain. At 10 × 8in, graininess begins to show, and larger prints will show it even more.

HOW BLACK-AND-WHITE FILM WORKS

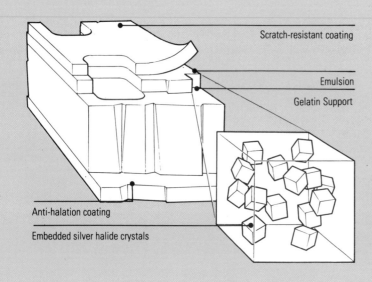

Scratch-resistant coating

Emulsion

Gelatin Support

Anti-halation coating

Embedded silver halide crystals

In black-and-white film, the active element is the emulsion – a thin layer of light-sensitive crystals of silver halide suspended in gelatin. This is spread on a tough, flexible but not stretchable base of cellulose-acetate. Protecting the delicate emulsion layer is a scratch-resistant coating, while under the base is another coating to reduce reflection of light back into the emulsion.

1 When black-and-white film is exposed to the light in the camera individual grains that are struck by light react, but invisibly. The mechanism of this reaction is rather more complicated than might at first be imagined, and is triggered by free independent silver ions and small specks of impurities such as silver sulphide. Some of the silver ions collect together at sites that have been exposed to light,

forming a latent image. It is called "latent" because, although real, it still needs the action of a developer to increase it in the order of about ten million times in order to make it visible.

2 Adding developer solution to the exposed film converts those silver halide crystals that contain silver ion traces into black silver metal. At this stage, which must be performed in darkness, the crystals that did not receive any light are still sensitive.

3 The final stage in the process is the removal of the developer and the addition of fixer, which turns the remaining silver halide crystals into salts that can be washed away. When this is complete, the image is stable and the film can be exposed to light without any further changes taking place.

OPPOSITE Using fast film does not always mean an unsatisfactory graininess as this example shows. Such a photograph would be impossible on slow film.

ABOVE LEFT On other occasions, you will need to photograph scenes that feature very high contrast; again, slow films' ability to handle high contrast makes them perfect for the job.

ABOVE RIGHT Certain scenes, such as this still-life set, demand that you use a film capable of rendering as much detail as possible. Because of their very fine grain, slow films – between ISO25 and ISO32 – are by far the best choice.

GRAININESS

Graininess is a purely photographic quality. It comes from the process of photography, and not from the scene or subject. Practically, it is one of the most important image qualities, and is more noticeable in a black-and-white picture than in colour. This is because the grains in a black-and-white negative are solid black, whereas developed colour film has instead overlapping patches of transparent dye in three hues, giving a less distinct effect. Whether you consider graininess as interfering with the image or adding to it is a matter of opinion, but how visible it is depends on the type of film, how you develop it, and the degree of enlargement.

RIGHT For most still life studio shots, graininess would simply be an intrusion, so slower film is the obvious choice.

ISO RATINGS

Compare the difference in graininess of these three films with different ISO ratings. The print (below left) was taken from the Plus-X film, which has the rating most commonly found.

Panatomic-X, ISO25; very fine grain.

Plus-X, ISP 100; medium grain.

Tri-X, ISO 400; fast, grainy.

ABOVE Graininess creates its own mood, as in this portrait, and should not thereforé be seen as inherently detrimental to good prints.

The picture above shows typical graininess – a speckled texture. What you see here, however, is not the individual grains themselves; they are far too small to be distinguished by the naked eye. Graininess is the appearance of clumps of many grains, overlapping each other in what is a relatively thick layer of emulsion. The grains are jumbled and stacked on top of each other. Nevertheless, graininess reflects granularity, which is the actual measurement of how prominent the grains are.

Graininess runs hand in hand with film speed, as is easy enough to see by making a direct comparison between slow, medium and fast film. Photograph the same scene with each in turn; with the only change to the camera and lens being the exposure setting. The difference in the finished print is obvious the greater the enlargement of the negative, the more noticeable graininess will be.

CONTRAST

The third related image quality is contrast. When used to describe the performance of a film, this is a measure of how the range of tones in the negative compares with the range of tones in the real scene. Although this is reasonably straightforward, contrast is highly manipulable.

Imagine a typical daylit scene, with a full range of intermediate tones, some shadows and some highlights (ignore the colours). With a meter, you could measure the range of tones; there would probably be a difference of several stops between the lightest and darkest parts. A film that, given the correct exposure, reproduces all these tones more or less exactly has medium contrast. This, indeed, is what happens with a regular medium-speed film: if you take care over the exposure,

Note how there is more shadow and highlight detail in the negative (right) than in the straightforward print produced from it (below).

processing, choice of paper grade, and printing, the final print should have the same tonal range.

However, contrast is linked to speed and graininess, and slow emulsions are more contrasty than fast. This is complicated a little by the processing stage: an extra-fine grain developer, or under-development with any other, tends to lower contrast, while high-energy developers or over-development increase it.

These contrast differences affect the negative image but, unlike graininess which is transmitted faithfully from the negative to the print, the amount of contrast also depends on the printing stage. In practice, contrast differences between types of film and methods of development are much less than those that can be made later, in the darkroom. As we will see in the section on printing, the selection of printing paper grade, dodging and burning-in techniques and print development can cover most of the film differences.

FILM FORMAT

The camera you use will determine the size of film you buy, and with 35mm there is no further choice. All 35mm cameras accept the single, standard film width, and with few exceptions (half-frame and panoramic models) the negative frame is a standardized 24 × 36mm, that is with proportions of 2:3.

With medium and large format cameras, however, there is often a choice of frame size, and this has a significant effect on the image quality. Graininess, as we saw earlier becomes apparent only beyond a certain degree of enlargement. If you normally print up to 8 × 10in, a 35mm negative will need to be enlarged 60 times to fill the paper, but a 6 × 7cm negative only has to be enlarged just over 12 times. At the extreme, a large-format 8 × 10in negative shot on a view camera would need no enlargement at all: it could be contact-printed for the finest image quality of all.

Different brands of film render colours differently, and it is up to you to make a subjective choice of which film you like best, based on your own personal experience and preferences.

COLOUR ACCURACY

Colour photography is made possible by the convenient fact that three primary colours, mixed in the right proportion, give a fair approximation of most other colours. They can even give an exact rendering of some colours, but not of all at the same time, at least not with the current state of the art in film technology.

Most of the time, colour accuracy is not an issue. It does become important with two kinds of colour: a group of hues to which photographic film behaves strangely, and what are known as recognition colours.

The first group includes dyes and surfaces that reflect strongly (but invisibly) in ultra-violet, far red and infra-red. Examples are blue morning glory flowers, and organic fabric dyes, particularly in dark green textiles.

The second set of hues, recognition colours, are those that the eye discriminates more sensitively than it does any others. They include grey, which is really an absence of colour, and very familiar ones, such as skin tones and the blue of a cloudless sky. Even a slight departure from an accurate version instantly looks wrong. A painted barn could be virtually any colour at all in a photograph: viewer would know if it were accurate only by holding the picture up against the real barn. A person's face, on the other hand, is an entirely different case: a pale complexion is already a delicate blend of hues, so that just a touch extra of green, for example, can make the subject of a portrait look ill!

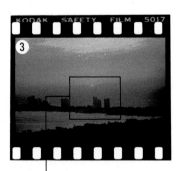

LEFT The pale image, weak shadows and green colour cast typical of film used long after the expiry date marked on its box.

37

Colour casts can be a particular problem with portraits, where a person can appear positively ill once the slightest shade of yellow or green is introduced! Here, it is important that the film is not out of date, and that light sources that may cause unpleasant casts (such as fluorescent lights) are kept well away.

RIGHT AND ABOVE RIGHT The danger with long exposures is that the reciprocity law between shutter speeds and apertures may be broken, resulting in a strong colour cast (right). It is possible to compensate for this, and most manufacturers can supply instructions as to the exact exposure adjustment required.

These are the inherent problems of colour photography that the film maker has to face, and generally they manage well enough. The main reasons why a photographer occasionally finds a colour cast over the image are that the film may be old, stored badly, or that a long exposure has caused a shift in the colour layers. When film ages, it turns towards one colour, often green, because the three colour layers in the emulsion become less sensitive at different rates. Long exposures cause a similar effect: the reciprocity between aperture and shutter speed (for instance, increasing one and decreasing the other by the same amount should give the same exposure) no longer works. The film becomes less sensitive at long exposures, but the three colour layers react slightly differently. Hence there is a colour shift.

ABOVE AND RIGHT A photo that may have taken ages to set up can often be ruined by the use of out-of-date film. Compare the photo taken using good stock (above) with the picture displaying the green cast, taken on aged emulsion (right).

MIRED SHIFT VALUES FOR KODAK FILTERS

FILTER (yellowish)	SHIFT VALUE	APPROX F-STOP INCREASE
85B	+131	⅔
85	+112	⅔
86A	+111	⅔
85C	+81	⅔
86B	+67	⅔
81EF	+53	⅔
81D	+42	⅓
81C	+35	⅓
81B	+37	⅓
86C	+24	⅓
81A	+18	⅓
81	+10	⅓
FILTER (bluish)	SHIFT VALUE	APPROX F-STOP INCREASE
82	−10	⅓
82A	−18	⅓
78C	−24	⅓
82B	−32	⅓
82C	−45	⅔
80D	−56	⅔
78B	−67	1
80C	−81	1
78A	−111	1⅔
80B	−112	1⅔
80A	−131	2

COLOUR TEMPERATURE

Both daylight and tungsten lights have what is known as colour temperature. This is a measure of the bluishness or reddishness of light expressed in degrees of temperature (Kelvins, which are similar to centigrade, but begin at absolute zero). Bluish light, as from a clear sky, has a high colour temperature; reddish light, like that from a low-wattage lamp, has a low colour temperature. Noon sunlight, for which daylight-balanced film is calibrated, is 5500K.

What makes colour temperature critical in photography, particularly indoors and in open shade outside, is that the eye quickly adjusts to differences. Film simply records what is there. The table shows the range of normal conditions, from candlelight to a deep blue sky. In ordinary pictorial photography, there are often no adjustments needed: a reddish sunset is expected and normal. On occasion, the colour cast can look inappropriate, such

COLOUR CONVERSION FILTERS

A wide range of filters is available to raise or lower the colour temperature of light reaching the film. The table below shows which filters you can use with which films to produce a normal lighting effect. Adding filters reduces the effective film speed.

Light source	5500°K	3400°K	3200°K	2900°K	2800°K
Film type Daylight	No filter	80B	80A	80A+82B	80A+82C
Tungsten type A	85	No filter	82A	82C+82	82C+82A
Tungsten type B	85B	81A	No filter	82B	82C

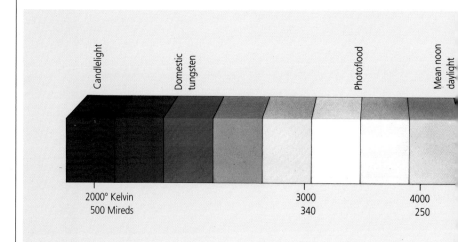

Candlelight   Domestic tungsten   Photoflood   Mean noon daylight

2000° Kelvin   3000   4000
500 Mireds   340   250

ABOVE The reddish light from a sunset is expected, and compensating for the colour cast with filters would make the scene look unnatural.

BELOW From the reflected light of a blue sky at this end to candlelight at the other end, this scale covers the range of colour temperatures most likely to be met in photography.

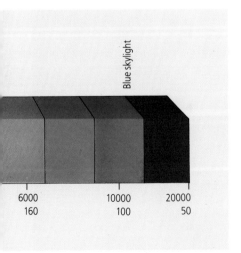

as a portrait taken under a blue sky in the shade of a building (the result will be too blue). Then, the answer is to use light-balancing filters over the lens, and in extreme cases of red/orange lighting, to switch to Type B film.

Calculations are often more convenient to make in the form of mireds (micro reciprocal degrees). These are the equivalent of one million divided by the Kelvin number, and are easier to use because they can be added and subtracted but stay constant. The table shows how they relate to filters, each of which has a mired shift value. Bluish filters (Kodak's 80 and 82 series) raise colour temperature and have negative mired values; straw- and orange-tinted filters lower the colour temperature and have positive mired shift values. For instance, if you were using Type B film, balanced for 3200K (312 mireds), but shooting by the light of a domestic lamp that gave 2900K (344 mireds), the way to correct the effect would be to use a filter with a value of minus

BELOW The orange cast achieved when using tungsten lighting while shooting on daylight-balanced film can have an unpleasant and undesirable effect.

32 mireds – in other words, a Kodak 82B or equivalent from another manufacturer.

Outdoors, the combination of a midday sun and some surrounding blue sky gives about 5500K, for which daylight film is balanced, and which appears 'white'. Earlier and later in the day, the sun is lower and some of its shorter bluer wavelengths are scattered by the atmosphere, making it more yellowish, orange and sometimes even red. Out of the sun, a blue sky has a much higher colour temperature, 10,000K and higher. Clouds, if continuous, usually raise the colour temperature slightly, perhaps to about 6000K, which is why a slightly warm-tinted filter, such as an 81B, can be useful.

3

PAINTING WITH LIGHT

AVAILABLE LIGHT

There is a wonderful variety to natural light, and knowing something of its ingredients and how they interact makes it possible to use daylight for photography with confidence. It is almost impossible to control (except on a small scale), but you can anticipate it, which is the next best thing. The two factors which control the quality of daylight the most are the position of the sun and the amount of diffusion by clouds, mist or haze.

The height and angle of the sun depends on the time of day, the season of the year, and on the latitude (it is highest in the tropics). On a latitude in the United States or most of Europe, there is a big difference between summer and winter. In the summer, the sun is high by mid morning and stays at its brightest until mid afternoon (once the angle of the sun is over about 40 degrees, it is fairly constant). However, in mid-winter, the sun never reaches even this height.

Probably the most valuable times of the day for general colour photography are the early morning and late afternoon into evening. Low, raking sunlight is especially good for revealing the texture of a landscape, and long shadows can help to pick out subjects dramatically against dark backgrounds. The low angle also gives the biggest choice of direction: by shooting into the sun you can create silhouettes, side-lighting gives good texture and contrast of detail, while frontal lighting, with the sun directly behind the camera, can give richly saturated colours. On top of all this, the sun moves relatively quickly at these times of day, so that within the

BELOW Early morning and late afternoon into evening are the best times for general photography. The texture of a landscape can be shown to its best advantage in low, reddish sunlight (below right), while reflections of low sunlight on water can lend atmosphere to an evening shot (below).

RIGHT The simplest solution to the problems of shadows in sunny conditions is to move your subjects into the shade, where the light is softer. Certain colour emulsions may give a very slight colour cast under these conditions.

	NATURAL LIGHT CONDITIONS			
CONDITION	GENERAL FEATURES	EFFECT ON CONTRAST	EFFECT ON SHADOWS	FAVOURED SUBJECTS
High sun	Difficult to add character to a shot	Low with flat subjects, high with subjects that have pronounced relief	Tall and angular subjects cast deep shadows underneath	Subjects that are graphically strong in shape, tone or pattern eg some modern architecture
Low sun	Great variety, depending on direction and weather; may be unpredictable	High towards sun, medium-low facing away	Strongest with sun to one side; least with sun behind camera	Most subjects suitable, particularly scenics
Twilight	Low light level only distinguishable when sky is clear	High towards light; low facing away	Shadows usually weak	Reflective subjects, eg automobiles
Haze	Enhances aerial perspective	Slightly weakens contrast	Slightly weakens shadows	Some landscapes, some portraits
Thin cloud	A mild diffuser for sunlight	Slightly weakens contrast	Slightly weakens shadows	Some portraits, some architecture
Scattered clouds	Dappled lighting over landscape, causing changing local exposure conditions	Slightly weakens contrast	Fills shadows slightly	Many landscapes
Storm	Unpredictable	Variable	Variable	Landscapes
Snowfall	Low light level; dappled foggy appearance	Weakens contrast considerably	Weakens shadows considerably	Landscapes, natural & urban
Moonlight	Very weak light, but quality similar to sunlight	As sunlight	As sunlight	Many subjects that would look too familiar in daylight

space of just one or two hours you can find a whole range of lighting conditions.

It is almost impossible to tell the difference in a photograph between sunrise and sunset, unless you know the actual scene. While sunset is usually a more comfortable time of day to work, the advantage of sunrise is that there are fewer people around, which is useful if you are shooting quiet landscapes. For an important picture, it is worth planning the camera viewpoint and the sun's position ahead of time; remember that the sun rises and sets at an angle, steeply in the winter, but nearly vertically in the summer.

A high sun is more difficult to work with, even though the middle of the day may well be the most convenient time for travelling and taking pictures.

Portraits are rarely attractive under a midday sun – the way that the shadows fall underneath, rather than to one side, is less flattering. Flat landscapes show very few shadows, and this lack of modelling can make them look dull and uninteresting, particularly at a distance. The most successful subjects for a high angle of sun are often those which already have strong shapes, strong structure or strong colours and patterns.

CLOUDS, MIST AND HAZE

Clouds alter the quality of sunlight by diffusing it, and also play an important role as components in a landscape. The extent to which they soften the light and reduce shadows depends on how thick the

OPPOSITE Although undeniably attractive, snow scenes photographed in strong sunlight can pose problems for built-in exposure meters. The meter may be fooled into under-exposure, reading the glare of the sunlight on the snow as the dominant lighting in the scene. Solutions include taking a separate exposure reading from the main subject – in this case the house – or taking an incident light reading with a hand-held meter.

A shroud of low, dense cloud diffuses light over the entire sky, occasionally to the extent where shadows disappear altogether.

45

ABOVE Look up, and adjust your composition to make the most of dramatic storm clouds.

RIGHT Low cloud on hilltops can soften light beautifully, providing the photographer with the perfect opportunity to exploit the naturally strong texture of the landscape.

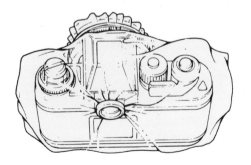

RIGHT The basic techniques for waterproofing a camera will also serve to keep out dust. Seal the camera in a plastic bag and secure with rubber bands. Use the open end of the bag for the lens, leave enough room inside to operate the controls and cut a small hole for the viewfinder, sealing it with another rubber band.

cloud cover is and on how high. So, a shroud of low, dense cloud diffuses light over the entire sky, to the extent that on a completely overcast day there are no outdoor shadows at all, and it may be impossible even to see the direction of the sun. Thin, high cloud, on the other hand, just takes the edge off shadows and highlights, and can help, for instance, in a very slight softening of a portrait.

As well as diffusing sunlight, cloud cover also reduces the amount, and this has an obvious effect on the exposure settings for the camera. As a rule of thumb, thin, high cloud can reduce the light level on the ground by up to one stop, a bright cloudy day has about a two-stop effect, moderately overcast about three stops, and strongly overcast (stormy) about four stops.

Although cloudy weather reduces local contrast by making the light more enveloping and weakening shadows, in a broad landscape it can actually increase the contrast between land and sky. There may be a modest difference in brightness between green fields and a blue sky, but it can reach up to five or six stops between the same landscape and a bright, overcast sky. In this kind of view, it can help either to use a neutral graduated filter or to give the sky extra exposure when making the print.

Clouds of different types and shapes can also make imposing parts of a landscape, and can even be dominant enough to make the main subject of a photograph. The most useful in this way, to be included as part of the composition, are those with distinct, precise shapes – fluffy cumulus, cirrus, or the anvil-shape of a thunderhead – and those with sharp tonal contrast.

In order to make the most of interesting clouds, it helps to use a wide-angle lens (to take in a broad sweep of the sky) and to place the horizon close to the bottom of the frame. Also, if the sun is more or less at right angles to the camera view, a polarizing filter will emphasize the contrast with the blue areas of the sky. The most useful filters of all for black-and-white photography, however, are yellow,

orange and red, which darken the entire blue of the sky to differing degrees.

PROBLEM LIGHTING

■ A MATTER OF BALANCE

One of the eye's remarkable qualities, not shared by photographic film, is the way in which it can accommodate different types of lighting. The colour of daylight varies with the weather and the time of day, and is in all cases very different from that of domestic lighting. Yet, we rarely notice the differences. Film is more rigid in its recording of colour, and in order for scenes to appear normal in a photograph, it is often necessary to use filters or to choose a type of film that is balanced for the particular light source.

Most colour films are, naturally enough, balanced for daylight. This is, after all, the light under which most photographs are taken. What this means is that a scene photographed on a sunny day will appear to be lit neutrally: whites will photograph

BELOW Two photos that show perfectly the problems and solutions encountered when working with tungsten lighting. One (left) shows the strong orange tint that results from shooting on daylight film a scene that is predominantly lit by tungsten (the household lamps in the background). The other photo (right) has a far more natural look, the result of using tungsten-balanced film. An alternative is to us a blue filter.

ABOVE This picture was taken on daylight film; the mixture of natural and tungsten light has given a slight orange cast to the meat. But it is precisely the richness and warmth of colour which gives the image its point, so why filter?

CENTRE Tungsten lighting is still the standard illumination for many interiors, and is invariably exposed to view rather than hidden. In this case, the presence of the candelabras has been exploited as a positive advantage.

white, greys remain pure, without a trace of colour, and flesh tones appear natural. Daylight-balanced films are the standard, and are made to record noon sunlight as white.

There is, however, another type of film, balanced for tungsten lamps which have a colour temperature of 3200K. This is much more orange than sunlight, as you can check for yourself by shooting an indoor, tungsten-lit scene with regular daylight film. Nearly all tungsten-balanced films are known as Type B. Type A, which is balanced for slightly less orange 3400K lamps, is now almost obsolete; a Type A Kodachrome is available in some countries.

■ TUNGSTEN LAMPS

Tungsten lamps are still the standard type of lighting in most domestic interiors, even though fluorescent strip lights are steadily replacing them in larger public areas and offices. Many restaurants also keep tungsten in preference to fluorescent because of the warmer, more friendly atmosphere it creates. The colour temperature depends very much

on the wattage of the lamps, and this is usually less than 2900K. So, even on Type B film, domestic tungsten lighting appears yellowish or orange.

To compensate for this warm cast, you would need a bluish filter in Kodak's 80 series when using Type B film. Either an 80C or 80D filter will give a reasonably neutral result, but with daylight-balanced film you would have to add an 80B on top of this. However, this kind of precision is not necessary; psychologically, a warm cast to a room is seen by most people to be quite attractive. If you are shooting colour negative film, a considerable degree of correction can be undertaken at the printing stage anyway.

What is usually more of a problem is the way that tungsten lamps tend to be positioned and used in interiors. More often than not, they are exposed to view rather than concealed (as most strip lights are used). This makes for high contrast, with pools of light, and there is often no way to avoid a bright

BELOW For street scenes at night you will need to use a tripod to prevent camera shake, and bracket exposures.

lamp appearing in shot. The best answer is to choose a viewpoint and composition that either hides a lamp from direct view behind some other object (such as a pillar or piece of furniture) or keeps it small in the frame.

Light levels from domestic tungsten lamps are low, and call for either a slow-to-medium film on a tripod, or a fast film if you want to shoot at speeds that will freeze normal movement and allow you to hold the camera by hand. For example, an average home interior with ISO64 film would need a setting in the region of ¼sec at f/2.8; with ISO320 film this could be 1/30sec at f/2 – just acceptable for a handheld shot. Remember that, if you are using a fast daylight-balanced film, adding a blue filter such as an 80B will cost some exposure – about 1⅔ stops. If you need to increase the possible shutter speed, uprate the film; ISO160 Ektachrome, for example, can be used at ISO320 if you push-process it by an extra stop.

■ FLUORESCENT LIGHT

The most common type of artificial lighting, both outdoors and indoors, is now fluorescent. The major problem for the photographer is that these strip lights do not reproduce on film the way they appear to the eye. The reason for this lies in the way they work. Inside the glass envelope, an electrical discharge causes the gas to glow, and a fluorescent coating to the glass helps to make this look white. However, the spectrum of light that it emits has gaps, particularly in the red end of the spectrum. The result is that, while the effect is visually close to white, on film it looks green.

This would not be so bad if all fluorescent lamps were consistently green. However, there are different types, a variety of brands, and they change colour with age. The only two ways of making sure of exact correction are to use a colour meter or to make a test with several filters. For most people, neither of these alternatives is really acceptable, so the standard solution is to use one basic filter and hope for the best. All major filter manufacturers supply a fluorescent-correction filter, which is close to magenta with a strength equivalent to about CC30 on the Kodak Wratten scale. In fact, with a set of three gelatin Colour Compensating filters – CC10M, CC20M, and CC30M – you can bracket exposures and be reasonably certain of a close match. As fluorescent lights are deficient in red, daylight-balanced film is a better choice than Type B, which needs stronger filtration and therefore longer exposures.

RIGHT Photographers wishing to use daylight-balanced film under tungsten lighting can avoid the green cast with the use of a simple filter, as shown here. Major filter manufacturers can supply a fluorescent-correction filter, which has a strength close to CC30 on the Kodak Wratten scale.

ABOVE A typical example of the sickly green cast that results from shooting with daylight-balanced film under fluorescent lights. Unfortunately, the lights are not consistently green, but vary according to make and age.

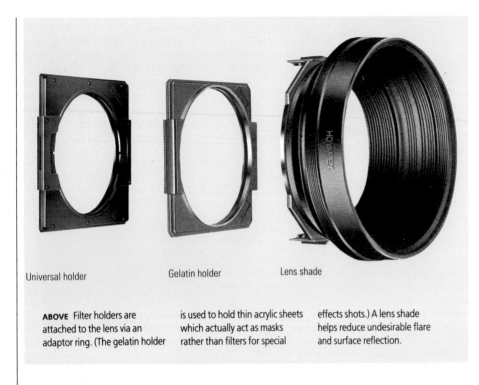

Universal holder

Gelatin holder

Lens shade

ABOVE Filter holders are attached to the lens via an adaptor ring. (The gelatin holder is used to hold thin acrylic sheets which actually act as masks rather than filters for special effects shots.) A lens shade helps reduce undesirable flare and surface reflection.

■ FIREWORKS

Fireworks are a form of flames, and easy to photograph very successfully if you take certain precautions. The chief thing to remember is that the shower of a bursting firework can only be captured with a time exposure. The shorter the exposure, the smaller and less impressive it will appear. The easiest way of setting up a firework shot is to choose a lens that encompasses the entire scene – the setting (which may include buildings in the case of a major firework display) and the entire height reached by the rockets. Watching a few go off first will help you establish your bearings. Then, you can lock the camera in position on a tripod, and wait. As you see the rocket rise, open the shutter, and leave it open until the last remnants of the burst have died away. You can even leave the shutter open to record several overlapping bursts. The aperture setting is rarely critical: with ISO 100 film, within a stop or so of f/4 will be fine.

ABOVE LEFT As a general rule, longer exposures result in more impressive photographs of fireworks.

ABOVE The cast caused by mercury vapour lighting need not be unappealing but if the photographer wishes to filter the cast out, either a CC30 red or CC40 red filter may be used.

FILTERS FOR COLOUR PHOTOGRAPHS

Filters that fit over the lens are a key method of controlling the colour and tone of your images. The important filters are not, however, the special effects and trick filters that produce rainbows, stars and drastic colour changes. Although these can sometimes be fun to experiment with, the filters for serious use are those that balance the light, compensate for shifts, cut parts of the spectrum and alter contrast. Few photographers maintain a full set, but it is as well to know which filter will do what.

■ LIGHT BALANCING FILTERS

This range of filters is used to match the film to the light. We have already seen why this is necessary in selecting daylight or tungsten-balanced film. However, you may often find yourself with the wrong film for the light source; for instance, if you have been using regular daylight film but suddenly find an opportunity for an indoor picture. In this case, there is a blue filter to balance the light – 80A in the Kodak series (there are equivalent filters from other manufacturers, with different designations). The opposite filter, for using Type B film in daylight, is an 85B. These two filters are the strongest that are normally used, but a whole range of weaker filters is available for making slight corrections. One of the commonest uses is on an overcast day, when the overall colour balance is a little cool. To warm up the image, many photographers use an 81, 81A or 81C filter. These are straw-coloured and give just a hint of warmth. Indoors, using available domestic tungsten lighting, cooling correction may be needed, as the colour temperature of these lamps is lower than the 3200K of type B film.

■ COLOUR COMPENSATION FILTERS

These filters are for correcting colour shifts – the kind that may be due to differences in film manufacture, reciprocity failure or to some artificial light sources such as fluorescent and vapour lamps. They are available in six basic colours: red, blue, green, cyan, yellow and magenta. There are different strengths for each, and in the right combination, any colour can be created.

■ ULTRAVIOLET FILTERS

These plain, or slightly yellowish, filters are designed to cut the response of film to invisible UV wavelengths. These wavelengths make distant haze appear bluish and add a blue cast to pictures taken on mountains. Improvements in recent years in film has made UV filters less dramatic in their effect on colour film, but still useful (they also protect the front of the lens).

■ POLARIZING FILTERS

Daylight is partly polarized, which means that it vibrates in only one plane. Although this effect is normally invisible, it can be used by means of a polarizing filter, which allows light through in just one plane. If the plane of the daylight and that of the filter are lined up, there is no effect, but if the filter is rotated, it quenches the polarized light. In practice, this affects reflections from anything

BELOW AND BELOW RIGHT
Ultraviolet light can make distant haze appear bluish. A UV filter can correct this.

A polarizing filter was used for the shot on the left, which cut out the reflection from the surface of the water; but the effect is unsatisfactory because of the lack of light altogether. The shot without the filter (below left) is probably better. Filters will not solve every problem.

RIGHT Since the blue of a clear sky is caused by light being reflected off tiny particles in the atmosphere, that blue can be deepened with the use of a polarizing filter.

except metal, and the most obvious effects are when photographing water or glass. If the camera view is about 35 degrees, the surface reflections will virtually disappear. And, as the blue of a clear sky is caused by light being reflected off minute particles in the atmosphere, the blue is intensified by the filter. This sky-darkening is strongest at right angles to the sun, and weakest in the direction of the sun, directly away from it, and close to the horizon. An especially useful application of polar-

HOW FILTERS WORK

These diagrams (below) show how coloured filters subtract from basic white light. The three filters are of the complementary colours, yellow, magenta and cyan. The yellow filter blocks the path of the blue light rays, allowing red and green to pass unhindered. In the same way the magenta filter blocks green light rays, and the cyan filter blocks red. When all three filters are combined together no light at all is allowed through, and the result is black. The two set circles show the two ways of creating colours photographically. The three primary colours – blue, red and green – when mixed equally, create white. In combinations of two they create complementary colours – blue and red make magenta, green and red make yellow, and blue and green make cyan. This is the additive process. In the subtractive process, complementary colours subtract from white light to produce the primary colours and black.

Additive process

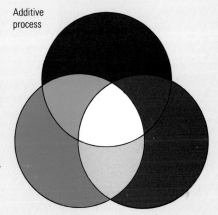

Subtractive process

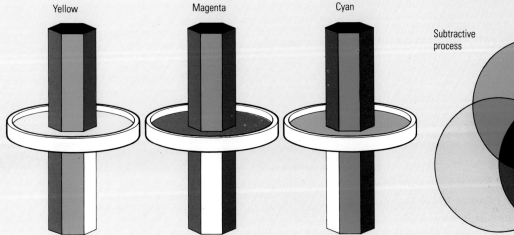

Yellow   Magenta   Cyan

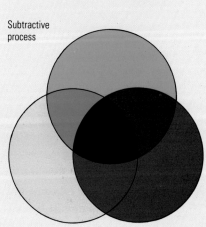

RIGHT The mottled glass of a diffusing filter is particularly effective in portraiture.

BELOW A graduated filter was used here to tone down the sky so that the buildings were not drowned by excessive contrast.

limit the depth of field to a narrow zone. Alternatively, you might want to introduce motion blur with a long shutter speed.

GRADUATED FILTERS

These very useful filters are toned over a part of the area, with the remainder clear. The division between the dark and clear halves is shaded gradually, so that in use there is no obvious line between the two.

DIFFUSING FILTERS

The glass in these filters is usually either mottled or etched in some way to break up the definition of the image slightly. The exact effect varies between makes, but in general they conceal detail (which may be useful in a portrait, to hide skin blemishes), and create a halo around subjects in backlit shots.

FOG FILTERS

Superficially similar to diffusing filters, these cut both colour saturation and contrast, in much the same way as real fog and mist. Some fog filters are graduated as well, so that just the upper half of the filter is affected; this can, with the right view, give a more natural treatment, with the fog appearing to increase with distance.

BELOW The atmospheric effect of the mist was enhanced with the aid of a graduated fog filter.

izing filters is in cutting haze in a distant view; they are much more effective than a UV filter. Polarizing filters absorb quite a lot of light, and the price to pay for using one is that you will need to adjust the exposure by about 1⅓ stops. A TTL meter automatically makes this compensation.

NEUTRAL DENSITY FILTERS

These are plain grey filters, in different strengths, and simply reduce the overall exposure to the film. As it is usually possible to do just this by closing down the aperture or shortening the shutter speed, they are not often needed, but can be useful if you have a very fast film on a bright day, or want to

FOG FILTERS

With filter A

With filter B

Fog filters can be of different strengths; the top picture, using filter A, is less affected than the one below, using filter B. They can be combined to produce an effect similar to dense fog. The effect can be varied by changing the aperture of the lens, but stepping down too far will tend to cancel out the filter.

A

B

NEUTRAL DENSITY FILTERS

With ND × 2

With ND × 4

With ND × 8

Neutral density filters are used to limit the amount of light entering the camera lens for three reasons: to adjust for the film speed (if, for example, you are using a very fast film on a bright day); to lower the shutter speed for special effects; and to decrease the depth of field.

ND × 2

ND × 4

ND × 8

DIFFUSING FILTERS

Standard

With Duto

Standard diffusing filters give an overall soft-focus effect because of their uneven surfaces. With the 'Duto' diffusing filter from Hoya, which has fine concentric lines etched onto it, the centre of the image remains sharp.

ADDING LIGHT

■ PORTABLE FLASH

Electronic flash is now the most common type of photographic lighting, and the standard unit is a portable flash that will fit on the camera body and work more or less automatically. Flash bulbs are much less used now that the electronic units are reliable and fairly inexpensive.

The principle of electronic flash is an electrical discharge passed through a glass envelope (the flash tube) containing a gas such as xenon. This gives a rapid pulse of light, useless for seeing by, but ideal for exposing film. All that the camera needs to do is to synchronize the opening of the shutter with the flash discharge. Although the flash pulse from a portable unit is usually very fast indeed – around 1/50.000sec – the shutter speed on a typical SLR must be considerably slower, between

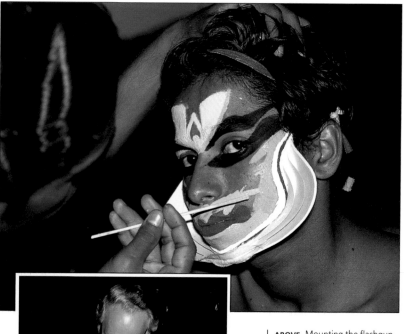

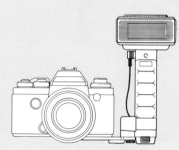

ABOVE Mounting the flashgun off the camera can eliminate the problem of red-eye.

LEFT Dedicated electronic flash has brought easy-to-use artificial lighting within the reach of every amateur.

FLASH ALTERNATIVES

Ring flash units (top) provide the even lighting necessary for macro-photography. The preferred flashguns of many photo-journalists, hammerhead off-the-camera units (bottom) are available with rechargeable battery packs (second from top). Although most modern guns have a bouncehead facility, the danger of red-eye is always present with hot-shoe mounted flashguns (third from top).

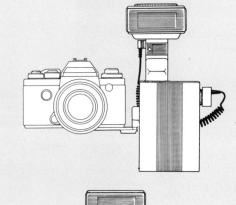

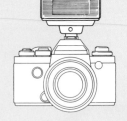

1/60 and 1/125sec on most models, and up to 1/400sec on a few. The reason for this is that the focal plane shutter on this kind of camera works at high speeds by passing only a narrow slit across the film. The near-instantaneous flash would expose only a narrow band – just the result if you set the shutter speed incorrectly. The 'X' setting on the shutter speed dial is intended for electronic flash synchronization.

Olympus have designed a special flash unit, compatible with some of the OM series of SLRs, which can be synchronized at all shutter speeds up to 1/2000sec.

■ GUIDE NUMBERS

The light output of a flash can be calculated in different ways, but for portable flash the usual method is a guide number. The higher the number, the more powerful the particular flash unit. The guide number is already given by the manufacturer, although, as it is usually calculated for use indoors, where the reflections from walls and ceilings add to the light, it is worth testing the recommended settings for yourself if it is not an automatic unit.

AUTOMATIC THYRISTOR FLASH

In common with all electronic flash units this portable model operates by converting low voltage from the batteries into a higher voltage, and storing the charge in a capacitor. When the unit is triggered, the capacitor, with the help of a smaller trigger capacitor, discharges the stored energy in a burst, ionizing the gas in the flash tube to produce a brilliant white flash. Automatic operation is made possible by using a light-sensitive photo-cell that measures the amount of light reflected back from the subject. This is connected to a thyristor – a very fast-acting electronic switch – which can cut off the supply of energy to the flash tube at any point. Modern 'dedicated' thyristor flash guns read the flash exposure through the lens, during the exposure, but require additional contacts in the camera hot-shoe to transmit exposure information. Most dedicated flash guns come from the camera manufacturers, though an increasing number can be adapted to a variety of cameras by changing the hot-shoe connector.

BELOW For cameras without a built-in hot-shoe (for instance, some Nikon models), a detachable hot-shoe can be fitted.

Adjustable diffusing head for different lens angles of view

Flash tube

Capacitor

Remote sensor, including photo-electric cell

Sync lead

Hot-shoe mount

Sync socket

Batteries (Alkaline or Nickel-Cadmium)

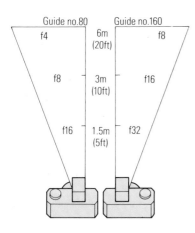

Guide no.80   Guide no.160

f4   6m (20ft)   f8

f8   3m (10ft)   f16

f16   1.5m (5ft)   f32

Particularly if you use a flash outdoors, without any bright surroundings to help, you may find that an extra half-stop exposure is needed. Guide numbers are given either in feet or in meters; to use them, simply divide the distance to the subject into the number and the result is the aperture setting. For example, if the guide number for the film you are using 100 (feet), and the person you are photographing is standing about 12 feet away, the setting should be f8.

■ DEDICATED FLASH

The easiest way of using flash is to buy a unit that is 'dedicated' to the particular make of camera. This type of flash is linked electronically to the camera's operation, and makes full automation possible, including through-the-lens automatic flash metering with some models.

Some flashguns have a zooming head which can be set to ensure optimum coverage for the angle of view of the camera lens in use – spreading the light output for a wide-angle lens, and channelling it for a telephoto lens. The zoom function is automatic on some models, according to how the lens is set.

■ BOUNCE FLASH

The very convenience of portable flash is also its major drawback. These units are designed to be triggered from the camera position, attached to the camera body by a hot-shoe, and although this makes them easy to use and handle, it is hardly ever the best position for a main light. Being so close to the lens, there are virtually no shadows, and the result is often flat in appearance, with little

FAR LEFT The marked difference in power between a flash with a GN of 80 and one with a GN of 160.

BELOW Bouncing flashlight off a suitably reflective surface can give results that are devoid of the harsh shadows that are a characteristic of direct flashlight. The loss of illumination in the average domestic room with a white, 10ft- (3m-) high ceiling will be in the region of two stops, and this should be taken into account when calculating exposure.

Direct flash without diffusion.

Direct flash with diffusion.

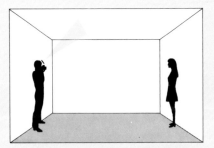

Flash bounced off ceiling.

in the way of modelling. An extra danger is the condition known as 'red-eye', in which light is reflected directly back from the retina of the person being photographed.

All this comes from having the flash on the camera and pointing directly forward. There are some situations which can benefit from this – notably subjects that have strong inherent colours and tones, but which are not shiny – but more often than not it is better to move the flash or modify its output in some way.

Many on-camera flash units have swivelling heads that allow the light to be aimed upwards. The idea behind this is to bounce the light off a ceiling; as most ceilings are white or lightly-coloured, effect is to soften the illumination on the subject. At the same time, the amount of light is drastically reduced, and you should be careful to watch for the under-exposure warning light (inside the viewfinder with a dedicated unit). In a typical domestic room, the ceiling will be about 10ft (3m) high and, if it is painted white, the loss of illumination should be in the order of about two stops. Remember, however, that for the metering to work, the sensor must be taking its reading from the subject rather than from the ceiling. So, unless the flash offers TTL metering, make sure that the sensor does not also swivel upwards.

To a limited degree, it may be possible to diffuse the flash. Some units have attachments available that act as reflectors: the flash is swivelled to aim up into a white chard. For others, an over-sized head can be attached with a translucent diffusing 'window' to serve the same purpose.

■ FILL-IN FLASH

A different use for on-camera flash is to counter the high contrast of a backlit scene by filling in the shadows. Without flash, there are just two choices

when the background is bright and the subject in shadow: setting the exposure to record detail in the subject (which will leave the background overexposed and washed out), or exposing for the background (which may leave the subject almost in silhouette). If it is important to have both well-exposed, fill-in flash is the answer.

The one important precaution is to make sure that the illumination actually does fit the description and 'fills' in the foreground shadows rather than takes over entirely. There is a temptation to use

Without fill-in flash.

FLASH OUTDOORS

Without the use of flash, backlit subjects (left) can be recorded as silhouettes, since the average SLR's metering system will record the bright sky as the dominant light source. Fill-in flash quite literally 'fills in' the details that have been lost in shadow.

61

too powerful a setting, but the result is distinctly artificial. As a rule of thumb, fill-in flash works best when it is not immediately obvious from the photograph that any extra lighting was used.

The simplest approach to calculating the amount of flash output is first to decide on the ratio of flash to daylight. A ratio of 1:2 is the absolute maximum; if the flash is any more powerful, the effect will be unnatural. A more useful ratio is around 1:4, which means that the flash output is four times (two stops, in other words) less than the level of the daylight. A more understated effect is possible with ratios of 1:6 and 1:8. Any ratio less than this and there is virtually no effect at all.

Apart from those flash units that deliberately allow a fill-in setting, you can adjust the flash-to-daylight balance in two ways, either by altering the flash output or by altering the camera's aperture setting and shutter speed. Altering the shutter speed affects only the daylight exposure, not that of the flash, but there is an upper limit – the flash synchronization speed.

First take an exposure reading of the daylight level from the background. Set the shutter and aperture to give this. The job of the flash is now to boost the brightness of your shadowed foreground subject, so first calculate from the distance what the aperture setting should be for a full flash effect. For a 1:4 ratio, what you want is two stops less than this. So, if the reading from the background is 1/125sec at f/11 and the full flash setting for the subject works out at f/8, you would need to reduce the flash output by one further stop or make the aperture smaller by one stop. One answer here would be to shoot at 1/60sec at f16; another would be to lower the flash output, either by its output

LEFT The trick with fill-in flash is not to make it obvious; the viewer must be fooled into thinking that you photographed the scene as you saw it. To achieve this, a clever balance must be reached between the fore- and background lighting.

BELOW Off-camera flash is preferable in situations where time is available to assess both the viewpoint and the lighting. The light may either be bounced off a reflective surface or passed through a diffusing material.

selector (if it has one) or by covering the head with a neutral density filter or a piece of white cloth with the flash unit on manual exposure.

■ OFF-CAMERA FLASH

In any situation where you have time to work out the viewpoint and lighting, it is nearly always better to move the flash off the camera, and hold it or position it separately. This calls for a sync lead, or, in the case of a dedicated unit, an extension cable to carry connections to all the contacts. A bracket that attaches to the base of the camera can make a small improvement, but if you are taking the trouble to set up an indoor portrait, it is often worth attaching the unit to a small stand or tripod. Then, the flash can either be bounced off any large, white surface – ceiling, wall, or large white card – or be diffused by aiming it through some transluscent material.

With these rather more advanced lighting techniques, a portable flash unit is by no means the only type of lighting equipment to consider. If you want to concentrate on indoor photography –

portraits, for instance, or still life shots – it is worth looking at the serious alternative: mains-powered flash. At the top end of the scale, large flash units designed for professionals are heavy and expensive, but there are many smaller units that are very convenient to use. The big advantage of a mains-powered flash is that the output can be much higher than that of a portable unit. Another advantage is that the recycling time can be in the order of a second or two.

STUDIO LIGHTING

The beauty of working in a studio is that the photographer has total control over lighting, and is not at the mercy of the vagaries of weather.

Mains-powered studio flash units work on the same general principle as a portable flash, although on a larger scale. The flash head is usually larger, and is intended to be used with some kind of fitting: bowl reflectors or screens and boxes that diffuse the light. Because they are rarely used as direct, unmodified lighting, the idea of guide numbers is not particularly useful – the illumination depends on the type of reflector or diffuser. Instead, these units are rated in terms of their electrical output, in watt-seconds, also known as joules. There is no simple way of using this rating to work out the aperture setting, but in indoor photography, most photographers who regularly use flash quickly become familiar with certain lighting set-ups, for which the exposure settings are consistent. In any case, if you go to the trouble of investing in a mains-powered flash, it is worth also buying a flash meter.

Always make the photographic lighting that you use do what you want, rather than accept the limitations of its design. For example, just because a flash unit comes with a small bowl reflector does not mean that it should be used always like that. Instead, think of the light as a raw material – a basic supply of illumination that must be modified to produce the required results. There are three basic things that you can do with a lighting unit: reflect it, diffuse it, or concentrate it.

■ REFLECTION

The basic principle for softening shadows and making the illumination more even is to make the light source broader. One of the simplest ways of doing this is to bounce the light off a large, plain white surface. What happens is that, instead of the

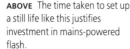

ABOVE The time taken to set up a still life like this justifies investment in mains-powered flash.

subject being lit by the direct beam of the flash, it receives its illumination from the reflector. This is the principle behind tilting a portable flash head upwards to the ceiling, but there are many other possibilities. White cards, paper or cloth hung up in appropriate positions can be reflectors, as are photographic umbrellas. The umbrellas are available in different materials: silver gives a more intense and concentrated light, while gold, for example, adds warmth.

DIFFUSION

Reflectors, although inexpensive and easy to assemble, have two disadvantages: they cannot always be suspended or positioned in exactly the right place, and they absorb a lot of light. An alternative is to shine the light through a diffuser. This can be any translucent material, such as tracing paper, thin white cloth, milky plastic, or anything similar. The most basic way of doing this is to put the light on a stand, and hang the diffusing sheet

BASIC STILL LIFE LIGHTING

For small objects without backgrounds, a simple set that gives consistently good results can be built with a table, clamps and a smooth, flexible white surface such as formica. The white sheet propped against the wall so that it falls into a natural curve, gives an even, seamless background to the shot.

BELOW Suspending a 'window' light directly overhead suits these Victorian dolls perfectly – their heads and bodies are clearly lit against the shadowed background, while the skirts are well illuminated by reflected light from the white surface. A lower camera angle would show less white foreground, and a higher viewpoint less of the dark background.

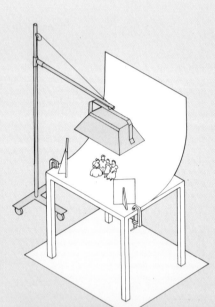

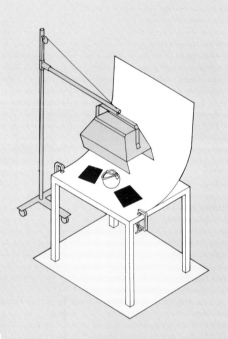

The subtle variations of colour in the glass of this Roman glass bowl (below) were best captured by backlighting, but for texture top-lighting was also necessary. A window light was aimed at the background, but adjusted so that a little spilled onto the bowl (above). As it was eventually to be printed as a cut-out, the edges of the glass could be defined by black card placed close-to.

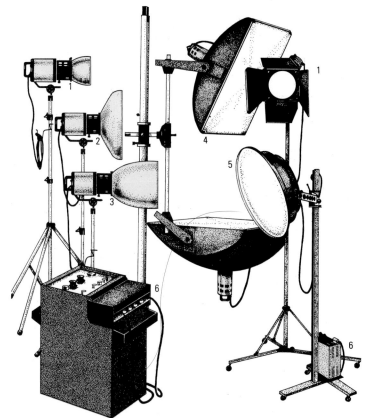

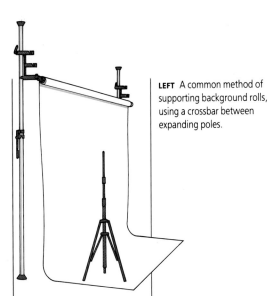

LEFT Good lighting is essential for photography – a typical set of equipment includes a standard reflector (**1**), narrow angle reflector (**2**), soft light reflector (**3**), a hazy light (**4**), a rondo light (**5**) and the power pack (**6**).

BELOW One of the simplest ways to broaden the light source is to bounce it off a large, plain white surface. In this case, studio umbrellas are being used, although everyday objects such as white cards, cloth or even newpapers can suit the purpose.

in front of it. For more control in positioning, however, the diffuser should be attached to the light. Mains-powered flash units have a fitting that allows this, but with a portable flash you may need some ingenuity as well.

■ CONCENTRATION

Although a naked lamp produces hard shadows, it is not a controlled beam. For certain kinds of shot a spotlight effect is useful, and for this the beam needs to be constricted. Lens attachments do this very well, but a cheaper alternative is to make a cylinder of black card and attach this to the front of the light. If it tapers slighty, so much the better.

■ PORTRAITS

The lighting set-up shown here is probably the most reliable of any. Most portaits are taken with the idea of making the sitter look as attractive as

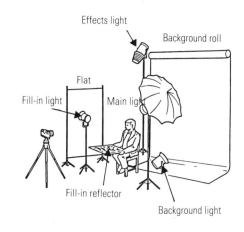

RIGHT A typical lighting set-up for a head-and-shoulders portrait; the umbrella diffuses the main light, and the fill-in light is bounced off a large white board. The effects light is fitted with a 'snoot' to concentrate the beam. The background light gives a graduated effect on a seamless roll of paper.

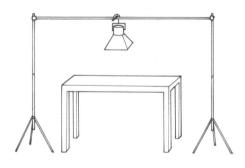

possible, and the quality and direction of the light can help enormously. If, for example, you are trying to convey the sense of character in a deeply lined face, you might consider harder lighting.

The main light is softened by using a reflecting umbrella, placed in a three-quarter position on a stand. This light gives the basic modelling. On the opposite side, a second light is used to fill in shadows, and is bounced off a larger reflecting surface so that its effect is both softer and weaker. Other optional lights are used to light up the background separately, and to highlight the hair.

■ STILL LIFE

Good still-life photography depends very much on precision in the lighting – exact control to suit both

the ideas of the photographer and the particular qualities of the object. Many still-life photographers use a 'window' light to give a type of diffusion that has soft but distinct shadows. These can be bought from photographic dealers, or made from wood, card or metal. Essentially, it is a kind of box, fronted with a textureless sheet of diffusing material. More often than not, the most appropriate position is over the subject, for which a boom lighting stand or a kind of 'goalpost' arrangement is useful. By varying the position of this single light, a surprising range of effects is possible. Note that, because the box-like fitting encloses the light, it can safely be used only with a flash unit, and will not work with one of the incandescent lamps described on the following pages.

The diffused illumination from a 'window' light should give soft but distinct shadows (top right). The softer light is ideal for still life work when reflective subjects are involved (top left). A common technique is to use the 'window' light to backlight a still life set (above left).

ABOVE Window lights can either be bought ready-built from photographic dealers, or constructed at home from wood, card or metal. The result should resemble a kind of box, fronted with a sheet of diffusing material.

■ TUNGSTEN-LIGHTING

Incandescent lamps, or 'hot' lights as they are sometimes called, have for long been the mainstay of photographic lighting. Even though they have now been largely superseded by flash in most situations, they remain irreplaceable for certain types of photograph.

All lamps that work by burning a filament are incandescent. The most familiar are domestic tungsten lamps, but those designed for photographic use burn more brightly. Some of the more intense ones use a quartz-like envelope instead of regular glass, and use halogen gas to prevent darkening with age and use. The colour temperature is usually 3200K, but sometimes 3400K. They are normally used with Type B film, although using a blue acetate sheet in front of the lamp can convert the light to the colour of daylight.

The output is measured in terms of the power drawn. The weakest operate at about 275 watts, but wattages of up to 1000 are common. The brighter the lamp, the hotter it is in use, and this kind of lighting needs care. In particular, it is dangerous to surround and enclose a lamp in some of the ways that flash units allow. Voltage fluctuations cause differences in the colour temperature, and a drop of 10% is likely to lower the colour temperature by about 100K. The more sophisticated studio lamps have adjustable flaps close to the front of the unit; known as 'barn doors', they can be used to prevent light spilling out in unwanted directions.

Unlike flash, tungsten lighting is continuous, and one of the things that makes it so easy to work with is that you can see exactly what lighting effect will be caught on film (with portable flash you must either guess or rely on experience). They can be added to existing lighting, and the overall lighting set-up can be tuned by eye alone. For shooting room interiors, particularly large areas, they are without equal. Even if the depth of field must be good, and a slow film is being used, adjusting the exposure is simply a matter of leaving the shutter open longer; the alternative with flash is to fire it repeatedly, but the recycling time needed between each discharge can make this process even longer than a continuous-light exposure.

BELOW Tungsten is still without parallel when shooting room sets. Note the tungsten light sources in this scene include the household lights in the background.

TUNGSTEN LIGHTS

Lights are available with 'barn doors' (**1** and **3**), adjustable flaps that prevent light from falling in unwanted directions. 'Egg crates' (**2**) make for a more directional tungsten light. Tungsten lights are available with a bar to conceal the lamp (**4**).

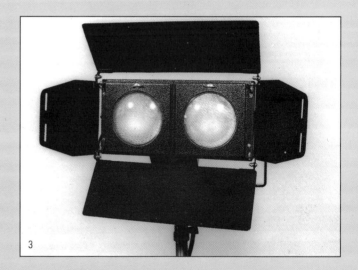

4

THE MONOCHROME IMAGE

A CRAFTSMAN'S FILM

Black-and-white film occupies a special, and unusual, place in photography. If you think about it dispassionately, it might seem that black-and-white is simply a poor relation of realistic colour, and that there is no very good reason for continuing with a medium that is outdated.

Certainly no-one invented black-and-white film and paper because they offered anything more than colour emulsions. In the nineteenth century, photography began with black-and-white because it was the only thing possible. There is little doubt that, had the chemistry been within the scope of the then current technology, colour would have been there from the start, and black-and-white imagery would in all probability never have emerged. A monochrome picture is relatively simple – indeed, the starting point for colour film also, which is composed of three layers of black-and-white emulsion with the addition of coloured dyes.

Nevertheless, black-and-white so dominated the early decades of photography that it became established, and acquired its own traditions. When colour arrived, it inevitably replaced the monochrome image for most of the photography market, but black-and-white had already made enough of a mark that it became as it now remains, the medium of the craftsman.

What black-and-white offers is a kind of refinement. Without hues, the image is thrown back on fewer graphic qualities, and these must be used more carefully to make successful pictures. Even more important is the matter of realism. Colour film has the possibility of reproducing, in two dimensions, every visual aspect of an occasion or view. Because of this many people expect no more of it than this: a record of things as faithful to the original as possible.

Black-and-white suffers from no such prosaic expectations. It can never be completely realistic, and this gives it the singular advantage of being able to be treated as a means of expression rather than just a documentary record.

LINE

In an image that must work with a single scale from dark to light, the basic graphic elements have a special importance. These are the components of all images; lines, shapes, forms, texture and the tonal range. Powerful black-and-white photography usually makes conscious use of one or more of these. The subject of a photograph may well be the most important and memorable part of the picture, but how you, the photographer, treat it graphically can make an enormous difference. It is even possible to make compelling images out of their design alone, with objects that are themselves of little interest.

The most basic of these elements is the line. It can be long, short, straight, curved, in different directions and of different thicknesses. Lines can separate the parts of a picture or join them, and they often have an irresistible tendency to pull the

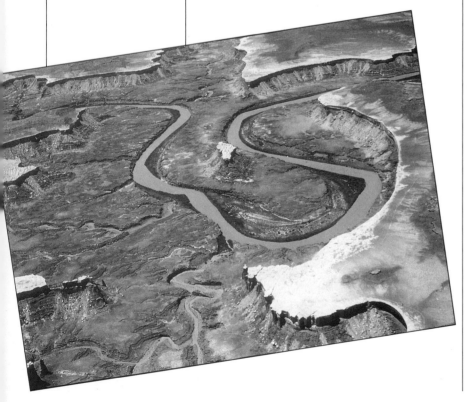

viewer's eye along, leading it from one area of the frame to another. While there is no pure, single line in nature (everything has some thickness and substance), they abound in images as edges and as connections between strings and rows of objects. The painted line on a road, the edge of a building, the horizon, and the stem of a tall plant are all obvious lines; the eye and brain, however, also make up lines from only a few clues. A row of soldiers on parade is interpreted as a line, but so is the direction in which a moving object travels. Even the direction in which a person looks can be interpreted as a kind of line.

Lines can have an understated psychological effect, giving a sense of movement or an impression of mood. For instance, horizontal lines tend to produce feelings of stability and solidity, while vertical lines have rather more energy. Diagonals have the most sense of movement, instability and dynamism. Curves also have some of the diagonal's movement, but temper it with a feeling of smooth gentle progression. Much of this stems from the experiences that certain lines conjure up. Gravity has much to do with the different sensations from horizontal and vertical lines; flat surfaces are bases, and supports for objects.

SHAPE AND FORM

If lines are the basic element in the construction of an image, the next level up is a combination of lines that encloses a particular shape. An enclosing set of lines is called, appropriately enough, an outline, and it is this that creates shape. Shapes exist in two dimensions, on flat images rather than in the real world: they are the projections of things, lacking volume. In other words, they are constructed by the eye, and are important as recognition symbols in human vision. How effective they are can be seen in the ease with which we can understand a complicated object from only a simple silhouette – the profile of a person's head, for example, is recognized as such.

In fact, not only is a silhouette the most exact and pure version of a shape – it is also one that black-and-white photography is particularly well suited to recording. Silhouettes are the product of high contrast due to back-lighting: typical examples include a tree on the brow of a hill against a dusk sky, or a figure standing in an open doorway seen from inside. Anything that heightens the contrast between the subject and its bright background will

ABOVE Exploiting lines can be a matter of being aware of potential. Here, the converging guitar necks draw the eye, and tipping the guitars towards the viewer has given the picture further punch.

BELOW Even if a certain amount of detail can be seen in the negative, it is possible to enhance the silhouette effect by choosing a hard, contrasty paper at the printing stage.

LEFT The two-dimensional nature of shapes in black-and-white photography means that you must adjust the way you view a three-dimensional world.

RIGHT Any distinct tonal contrast in black-and-white photography throws shapes into prominence. Shapes can be made the focus of the image in the darkroom by deliberately seeking out the juxtaposition of dark and light.

enhance the effect, and there are more opportunities for this with black-and-white emulsions than with colour. The exposure is important – not so full that it records details within the silhouette – but even more can be done in the printing, by choosing a 'hard', contrasty grade of paper. Indeed, a perfect silhouette is always possible by using lith film; this can be used for the original photography, or it can be used later, to make a conversion of a more normally toned original.

To a lesser degree, shapes in black-and-white photography are thrown into prominence by any distinct tonal contrast. Without resorting to any darkroom manipulation, shapes can be made the focus of the image by deliberately seeking out the juxtaposition of light and dark. The less convoluted the outline, the more the sense of shape will be apparent and will come through.

Because shape in photography is the projection of an object onto a flat surface, the orientation and the camera viewpoint alter our perception of things. A spoked wheel seen flat-on is perfectly obvious, but on the other hand, seen end-on is hardly recognizable. This is not necessarily a problem, but if you intend to use shape as an aid to recognition in a picture, give some thought to which angle gives the clearest view.

From shapes, one step further towards realism is form. This is the volume of an object, a sense of its three-dimensionality. Whereas it takes our familiarity and imagination to construct the depth and tangibility of an object from its shape alone, a photograph with a good sense of form makes this obvious by the distribution of tones.

ABOVE Still life photographers, whose success depends upon their ability to match lighting sets to subjects, are particularly concerned with form.

73

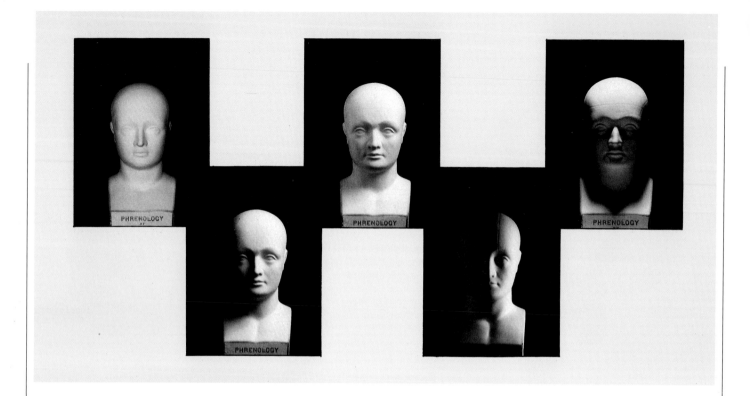

ABOVE Proof positive that our eyes use shading as the most vital clue to form. Simply adjusting the position of the light in relation to the subject alters the perception of it completely. From fairly straightforward frontal lighting (top row, left) to top lighting (top row, right), from hard lighting from a single side (bottom row, left and right) to off-centre top lighting with a reflector (top row, centre), basic adjustments to a lighting arrangement can drastically alter the impression given by an image.

LEFT Diffused sidelighting is ideal for conveying a sense of form, producing as it does relatively gentle transitions from highlight to shadow.

In fact, a number of techniques combine to convey form, not the least of which is lighting. Still-life photographers, whose success depends largely on their ability to design lighting sets that are appropriate to particular objects, are among those most concerned with form. The approach of an experienced professional to a new subject for a study is first a careful examination to appreciate the kind of volume it has. To take objects at random, a fist, a coin and a delicate orchid have clearly different forms, and each therefore, will need a different lighting approach.

While form should not necessarily dictate the lighting treatment, it is essentially an attribute of realism. A strong sense of form normally goes hand in hand with clear, unambiguous representation. Techniques that aid abstraction, such as those to enhance a silhouette, work against form. The class of lighting that usually best conveys depth and volume is that of moderately diffused side-lighting. With this, the gradation of tones across the surface of an object produces relatively gentle transition from high-light to shadow.

Our eyes use shading as a clue to the form of something. As long as the light source seems to be in a conventional position, the brain calculates from the play of tones across the surface what the projections and depressions are. A useful experiment is to take one object, one light, and make minor adjustments to the position of the light and to the level of diffusion, making a series of comparative photographs of the object.

TEXTURE AND TONE

Texture is the surface quality of an object and, like form, is distinctly three-dimensional. While it can be used in making abstract images, its principal value in photography is as an aid to conveying realism. In many kinds of shot, one of the aims is to get across to the viewer as close a representation as possible – to make it almost tangible. If the texture comes across strongly, this helps the sense of realism enormously.

Food photography, for example, needs all possible help to convey taste (itself not a visual quality in any way). Texture, because it is related to taste, nearly always plays an important part, and photographers who specialize in food normally take great pains with the lighting to reproduce tactile sensations – the crumbling roughness of pastry, or the glaze on a roast ham.

Lighting is the key to texture just as much as it is to form, although the techniques are different. Textures also vary enormously, not only from rough to smooth, but in individual character: the leather binding of a book and the surface of smooth sand, for example, may share a similar degree of roughness, but they are immediately distinguishable in a photograph.

For fine texture, the strongest impression of relief comes from very low, direct illumination that just skims the surface. Revealing texture in black-and-white is largely a matter of using the lighting to throw shadows. Fine texture needs hard-edged shadows to be distinct, and for this the light source needs to be naked. Look at the effect of bright sunlight when it just grazes a wall.

The same hard, raking light applied to a rough, knobbly surface may sometimes throw too much of the texture into shadow. If the indentations are deep, a more diffused light is likely to give a better sense. Also, texture does not always need to be taken to the maximum in photography. There are occasions when a less definite texture is desirable. In portraiture, for example, while a lined, weather-beaten face may make a striking character study, a portrait that is supposed to flatter the sitter is not likely to get a good reception if it throws wrinkles into prominence! In fashion and beauty photography, much of the lighting technique is concerned with softening skin texture by diffusion, shadow fill, and a lighting direction that is fairly frontal. Even the finest skin contains some blemishes; these are a texture that is usually less than welcome.

ABOVE For a still life such as this, where texture is all important, it may be necessary to adjust the image's contrast at the printing stage to make the most of the picture. In this case, the contrast has been lowered in the finished print.

OPPOSITE Raking light applied to a knobbly, rough surface can throw too much of the subject's texture into deep shadow, ruining the picture in the process. As in the case of this photo of a crocodile, it's best to wait until the light becomes more diffused, either by waiting for cloud or placing the subject in the shade.

■ COLOURS INTO TONES

Because black-and-white film converts from real life into tones, these tones can be altered, more or less at will. All that is needed is a set of coloured filters – coloured more strongly than the correction and light balancing filters common to colour photography. By choosing an appropriate filter, you can selectively manipulate the various shades of grey in an image. This freedom to experiment with the tonal relationships in a scene is one of black-and-white photography's strong appeals.

Often, however, a filter may be needed simply to compensate for a deficiency in the way that a monochrome film records light. The shade of grey in which a particular colour records depends on both the intensity of the light and on the spectral sensitivity of the film. Red records paler than normal on the negative because film is relatively insensitive to it; in the print it appears dark. At the other end of the spectrum, blue, to which film is more sensitive than our eyes are, exposes strongly onto film, and so appears pale in the print.

FILTERING COLOURS INTO TONES

Each of the four distinct colours in this still life – green, red, blue and yellow – are susceptible to alteration by filters. With no filter used, the over-sensitivity of normal black-and-white film to blue and its under-sensitivity to red give pale tones to the cigarette packet and a too-dark version of the red Dutch cheese on the left of the picture. A yellow filter lightens the yellow cheese and darkens the blue design on the cigarette packet. An orange filter performs a similar function to the yellow, but more strongly. A red filter dramatically lightens the red cheese and darkens the blue packet. A blue filter turns the yellow cheese almost black. A green filter lightens the tone of the apple, but makes the red cheese appear black.

No filter

Wratten 8 yellow

Wratten 16 orange

Wratten 25 red

Wratten 47 blue

Wratten 58 green

No filter

Blue filter

The best, and by far the simplest, way of appreciating the dramatic changes that can be made to a black-and-white photo is to put theory to the test. Compare the sky in the unfiltered picture (top left) with the lacklustre sky in the picture taken using a blue filter (top right). Then note how using a yellow filter (bottom right) has restored the blue to an acceptable strength. Finally, compare the unfiltered picture with the red filtered shot (bottom left); the extremely dark sky produced by using a red filter may not be to everybody's taste.

Red filter

Yellow filter

FILTER CHECKLIST FOR BLACK-AND-WHITE FILM

All the filters below, except the polarizer, are available in either glass or gelatin. As the glass thickness can distort, high optical quality is important in a filter, and this is expensive. Gelatin filters, on the other hand, are too thin to affect the optics of a lens, but must be handled carefully to avoid marking.

FILTER (KODAK WRATTEN NO)	EFFECT	USE	FILTER FACTOR*	ADDITIONAL F STOPS*
Yellow 8	Absorbs UV and some blue	Darkens blue sky to an acceptably normal tone, accentuating clouds. Lightens foliage	2×	1
Deep yellow (18)	Absorbs UV and most of the blue	Similar to yellow but with a more pronounced effect. Also darkens blue water and lightens yellow subjects, such as some flowers	4×	2
Red (25)	Absorbs UV, blue and green	Turns blue sky and water very dark, increases contrast and deepens shadows. Cuts haze and lightens red objects. In portraits, lightens lips and skin blemishes	8×	3
Green (58)	Absorbs UV, blue and red	Lightens foliage and slightly darkens sky. Makes red objects darker and deepens skin tone in portraits	8×	3
Blue (47)	Absorbs red, yellow and green	Lightens blue subjects, increases haze in landscapes	6×	2½
Neutral density	Absorbs all colours in equal proportions	Reduces exposure, enabling a slower shutter speed or wider aperture to be used	Various	Depends on which filter factor
Polarizing	Controls reflections and darkens blue skies at right angles to the sun	Can eliminate reflections when photographing still water and windows. Darkens blue skies under some conditions.	2.5×	1½
Ultraviolet	Absorbs ultraviolet	Cuts haze in landscapes, giving sharper image with better colour saturation	·	

*This list of filter factors and the related increase in aperture is based on normal daylight. When the colour temperature changes, in the evening, for instance, these factors will change.

Coloured filters provide the necessary contrast control in black-and-white photography. The tomato appears light on the left-hand side of the picture, because a red filter was used. Compare this with the opposite side of the picture, where it is the lettuce which is lighter, the result of a green filter being used.

ABOVE A red filter holds back green.

ABOVE A green filter, being the complementary of red, passes green but blocks red.

5

WORKING WITH COLOUR

CHOOSING EXPOSURE

How much you can rely on the TTL metering system in your camera depends on the sophistication of the equipment. Currently, the most advanced technique is multi-pattern metering, in which the picture area measured by the camera's meter is divided into segments. Each of these segments is metered individually, and the pattern is then compared with similar patterns already programmed into the electronic memory. Certain patterns usually indicate types of lighting condition (a dark centre and bright surround is typical of back-lighting), and the exposure circuits react accordingly). But in spite of the potential of advanced technology, the foolproof method of getting the exposure you want is to know yourself more or less what it should be. To do this, practise taking readings, either with the camera's meter set to manual, or with a hand-held meter as a back-up.

AVERAGE READINGS

This is the standard method – an overall reading that averages everything in the shot. It usually works. One precaution in a scene with a bright sky is to meter the view below the skyline. Most TTL meters are biased for this anyway, but with a hand-held meter, shade the top with your hand.

KEY READINGS

With this technique, you choose in advance the most important tone in the scene, measure that, and set the exposure to suit. Several cameras with TTL metering have this option, using a small central area (or spot) of the viewfinder. Otherwise, the classic method is with a spot meter, which measures over a one degree angle of view. Doing this, you can ignore a strongly contrasting background.

RANGE READINGS

These are a kind of 'thinking version' of average

LEFT The best approach to low-contrast scenes such as this is to take an average reading. Since the vast majority of TTL meters built to cameras do this anyway, the risk of the exposure going astray for this type of shot is minimized. If a hand-held meter is to be used, shade the top with your hand (above) so that the reading is not overly influenced by the sky.

ABOVE Night shots are notorious for providing exposure difficulties. Here, it is advisable to bracket exposures, starting with a reading from the most important subjects and then bracketing, for example, two stops in either direction.

readings. The technique is to measure the brightest and darkest parts of a scene, excluding reflections and deep black. With an incident meter, measure the brightest lightning and the darkest shadow. Provided that the range between the two is no higher than seven stops for negative and five stops for slide film, the average of the two readings should give a reasonable exposure.

BRACKETING

Most professionals bracket exposures around what they judge to be the right setting. This involves taking a rapid sequence, changing the exposure between each by half a stop.

CLOSE-UPS

Close-up images have a special appeal in photography, because they open up a fresh visual area. The relative ease with which a camera can be used to probe small scales brings a world of patterns and scenes that we do not normally see. The small scale makes it possible to control the lighting exactly, whether using natural lighting, flash or photographic lamps. There are, however, some special problems and precautions.

Close-up photography begins at the point below

BELOW Normal lenses do not have the close-focus capability required for true macro photography. However, shots such as this are quite possible with normal lenses if extension rings or extension bellows are added.

BELOW The real attraction of close-up photography is the way it can open up a whole new world; objects or aspects of objects that may otherwise have been ignored take on a new light.

RIGHT In general, hot-shoe mounted flashguns are not suited to close-up work. Ring-flash units, which can be attached to the front of your camera's light, provide the even lighting necessary.

which a normal lens cannot focus. This is normally just a few feet, and the greatest reproduction ratio (the ratio of the image to the subject size) is about 1:7. To close in more needs either a supplementary magnifying lens attached to the camera lens, or some means of moving the camera lens forward from the body and away from the film plane. The choice of close-up equipment reflects this: there are supplementary close-up lenses for modest magnifications, macro lenses that have especially long focusing mechanisms, extension rings and extension bellows.

Extending the lens from the film is the basic way of getting a magnified image, but it also reduces the amount of light that reaches the film. So, the greater the magnification, the more compensation is needed, either by opening the lens aperture or by increasing the exposure time. Alternatively, increasing the strength of the light or bringing it closer will make up the difference.

In practice, the difficulty of working out this compensation depends on the kind of camera you use, and on the type of lighting. If you measure the light reaching the film, as does a TTL meter,

ALLOWING FOR THE LENS EXTENSION

The following formula gives the increase in exposure. Translate this into f-stops by means of the table below.

$$\text{Exposure increase} = \frac{(\text{Lens focal length} + \text{Extension}) \times 2}{\text{Lens focal length}}$$

Alternatively, if you use flash, position it according to this formula:

$$\text{Flash-to subject distance} = \frac{\text{Flash guide number}}{\text{Aperture} \times (\text{Magnification} + 1)}$$

EXPOSURE INCREASE AND F-STOPS	
EXPOSURE INCREASE	INCREASE IN F-STOPS
1.2	⅓
1.4	½
1.7	⅔
2	1
2.3	1⅓
2.6	1⅓
2.9	1½
3.2	1½
3.6	1⅔
4	2

the exposure settings will be accurate. Otherwise, some calculation is needed (see box). With flash, if you have a dedicated unit and the reading is made off the film plane, rather than from an epso, there are no problems. Otherwise, position the flash according to the formula given in the box.

COLOUR AS SUBJECT

There is an important difference between true colour photography and merely photographing with colour film. You can treat colour as no more than another quality that enters the frame, whether it is wanted or not: or you can consciously look for the relationships between colours, altering your viewpoint, composition, and even selecting what you photograph on the basis of colour values.

Many photographers who grew up working in black-and-white adapted to colour film by treating it only as a way of colouring the kind of picture that they had always been shooting. At the other extreme, some photographers are attracted by the sensuousness of colour, treating it as something almost tangible. Pete Turner is one of the best known modern photographers who uses this approach.

While both methods are perfectly acceptable, we will concentrate in this section of the book on developing colour awareness. More than most other visual qualities, colour needs a trained eye if it is to be caught and used in a photograph. The reason for this lies in our easy acceptance of colours. Almost too easily, we often respond to colours around us subjectively, without really thinking about them. This is fine for enjoyment of colour, but in order to select it and compose with it in a

LEFT A major problem encountered by photographers when beginning colour work is ignorance caused by over-familiarity; because we encounter certain colours every day of our lives, we tend to ignore their photographic potential. Here, a simple strong yellow has been used to completely dominate the scene, creating a very striking image.

ABOVE The contrast between powerful reds and blues has been further helped here by the photographer's use of a polarizing filter, which has deepened the blue of the sky even further. Using slower films in these circumstances will result in even richer colours.

camera's viewfinder, it is important to know how different colours interact, which hues are common and uncommon, and so on. As with music, concentrating on colour enables you to be much more sensitive to it and more discriminating.

There are several techniques for making colours strong and insistent in photographs. One of the most obvious is to choose lenses and viewpoints that allow you to be selective. As we have already seen, large-scale views are not usually strongly covered overall, mainly because there is a large mixture of objects. Flowers growing at the edge of a wood become lost as you step further back. Closing in has the opposite effect. For this reason, both a macro lens and a telephoto can be used to isolate one or two strong colours from duller surroundings.

The lighting also plays a key role. If you use flash or other photographic lamps, you have complete control, but even in natural light you have the important option of waiting for the right angle of the sun, or better weather conditions. Generally, the best conditions for showing a colour at its most intense are full lighting with the least shadows and least reflections. If you look back to some of the examples of sunlit scenes, you can see that backlighting in various degrees is strong on atmosphere

BELOW When using slide film, try underexposing by between one half and one full stop to increase colour saturation. To test this, shoot several frames of a single scene at various exposures; the darker ones will feature the more intense hues.

ABOVE AND LEFT Pure hues prove irrestistible for most photographers, as they tend to be untarnished by shades of grey or black. A reliable technique is to use a single strong colour to dominate the frame.

ABOVE Fit a macro lens and a whole new world of strong colour opens up before you. Using a close-up lens helps isolate one or two strong colours, and careful composition helps eliminate potentially distracting hues from the scene.

and depth, but weak on colour. Frontal lighting, however, with the sun behind the camera or slightly to one side, enhances colour richness. On the same principle, so does a camera-mounted flash, with the exception that a shiny surface is likely to throw back reflections that drown the colour.

Overcast weather that gives flat, diffused light can also give good colour intensity, simply because shadows and reflections are at a minimum. Because we are conditioned to think of dull light as being weak, the colour may not seem so strong, but, provided that you close in tightly on a single hue, it will be on the film.

Another control that you can exercise is over the amount of light – by means of exposure. As an exercise, take a bright, pure colour, and photograph it at several exposure settings. The darker exposures will be the most intense. Slide film is particularly good with this technique for increasing colour saturation.

Although strong colours have an immediate appeal, it can also be a short-lived one. Photographs that rely heavily on an intense area of colour often do not sustain a longer look. They depend on making a quick visual impact. The range of pure hues is limited, and this restricts the choice for exploring colour relationships.

In nature, most colours are impure, diluted with others and with blacks and greys to give a much more neutral range than the ones we have seen on the last few pages. Typical landscapes contain browns and other earthy colours, and greens tinged with yellows and blues. These 'broken' colours, as they are sometimes called, are subdued, but in some ways offer more interesting opportunities than strong primary hues. Because the palette is restricted, the eye becomes more sensitive to small differences between colours, and this subtlety becomes the main appeal.

As with images in strong colours, the most important step here is to train the eye to see a limited range within an overall view. Being selective in this case means composing an image to exclude flashes of brighter colour that would be distracting. Because most people find it natural, when thinking about colour, to go for the obvious and definite, it takes a conscious effort to be restrained. The result can be unexpectedly beautiful.

ABOVE Resisting the temptation to go for strong, vibrant bursts of colour can sometimes bring great rewards; the eye will appreciate the subtle changes in hue as it follows this crowd scene.

BELOW Urban centres can appear drab and colourless. For the photographer, however, this can be turned into an advantage; even colours that would appear mundane in the countryside, such as the mauve of this railway carriage, can be used to great effect in the city.

SUBDUED COLOUR

The palette of colours can also be limited by the quality of lighting, and this gives the photographer much more choice in the treatment of a scene. Outdoors, the angle of the sun, the weather conditions and the camera viewpoint all contribute to the effect. In addition, understated use of filters can be used to enhance the delicacy of some hues.

Any of the atmospheric conditions that screen a view, such as haze, mist, fog or smoke, drain some of the intensity of colour. At the extreme, a dense fog reduces the components of a scene to monochrome. Judicious choice of camera position can help in increasing the natural effect of haze and mist: shooting towards the light increases the scattering of light. If you also shoot without a lens shade, the flaring will further dilute colour intensity. The way in which the word 'atmospheric' is often used to suggest a heightened mood in a picture acknowledges this visual effect.

Even without the help of atmospheric conditions, the angle of the sun helps to control the colourfulness of a scene. Frontal illumination, with the sun or light source behind the camera, picks out hues very clearly. To achieve the opposite effect, use back-lighting by shooting early or late in the day, from a viewpoint facing towards the sun. The effect

ABOVE A natural atmospheric condition such as haze can be further aided by the use of a soft filter to dilute colours.

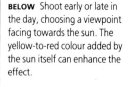

BELOW Shoot early or late in the day, choosing a viewpoint facing towards the sun. The yellow-to-red colour added by the sun itself can enhance the effect.

is enhanced by the yellow-to-red colour that the low sun itself adds to the image.

Filters can mimic some of these effects; it is, in fact, much easier to dilute an image than it is to sharpen it, in detail, tone and colour. A mildly coloured filter has the effect of adding a slight wash to the photograph, without making it obvious that the photographer is manipulating the image. Any of the several softening filters – diffusers, soft-focus, fog, pastel, and so on – have an effect similar to backlit haze and mist.

COLOUR ASSOCIATIONS

A quite different way of combining colours is across the colour wheel. Any two colours that are directly opposite each other on the wheel have a special relationship to each other; if a painter were to mix them, they would produce a neutral tone, or if two lights of these colours were played onto the same surface, the result would be white. On the face of it, this relationship may seem to be more important to a painter than to a photographer,

THE COLOUR WHEEL

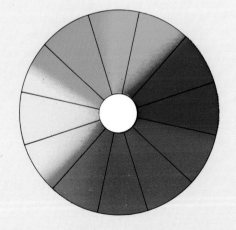

This is really a simplified spectrum bent into a circle. As well as a guide to colour relationships as seen by the human eye, the colour wheel helps to explain what actually happens during colour reproduction. Any three equally spaced colours (blue, green and red for example) combined equally give white. In the subtractive process white light is selectively blocked by dyes or pigments: thus a yellow dye will block blue light, which is opposite yellow on the wheel.

ABOVE Attractive images can be formed from the variations in shade of a single secondary colour, in this case green (a mixture of yellow and cyan).

TOP This combination of magenta and red has been aided by the muted atmosphere of the shot.

but in fact it underlies the harmony of what are called complementary colours.

To get a completely balanced effect using complementary colours, consider the relative brightness of each. Just a glance at the wheel shows that yellow is the brightest of the colours, and violet the darkest. So, to create an overall harmony in a picture that has these two complementaries, there needs to be considerably more of the violet than of the yellow – 4 to 1, in fact. In an orange and blue combination, the orange is brighter, although not to such an extreme degree; here, the harmonious relationship is about 3 to 1. Red and green, the final complementary pair, are evenly matched in brightness, and so combine perfectly in equal amounts.

Using viewpoint and focal length, it is often possible to frame a scene so that the colours are in particular proportions. This makes a very good exercise in working with colour relationships, but beware of thinking that there is something 'correct' in the combinations described here. There is nothing to prevent you from making a dramatic combination of colours that clash. Knowing these complementary relationships, however, will help you in deciding the amount of harmony or discord in a scene.

One of the most exciting parts of colour photography lies in the relationships between different hues. Most of the examples that we have seen in the last few pages have relied essentially on a single colour to carry the image. However, the sensation created by a colour changes when it is in the presence of other colours. Some blend together, others create tension, but all interact in some way. Knowing something of the theory of colour combinations will allow you to take extra control.

The basis of colour relationships is the colour wheel, used in one form or another by artists for centuries. This is closely, although not exactly, related to the spectrum of colours that can be seen in a rainbow, or whenever else white light is broken up into its parts. Imagine the spectrum that you can see being bent round so that it forms a circle of colour, like the one shown here. Going clockwise from red – one of the primary colours – the colour wheel progresses to the other primaries, green and blue, by way of the secondary colours in between. The way that this colour wheel is arranged is such that if all the colours are combined, they make white in the centre, and if any two opposite colours are combined, they too produce white. Opposite colours on the wheel are called complementaries.

RIGHT Although it is undeniable that strong primary colours are attention-grabbers, muted secondary colours used in the right combination can be equally effective.

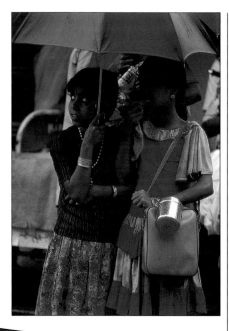

RIGHT Complementary colours can be employed even in subdued conditions to lift a photo above the ordinary.

BELOW The relative brightness of complementary colours must also be taken into account when composing a scene; in this case, the potential strength of the yellow has been off-set by the depth of the blue.

ABOVE An image can be given an extra boost by playing off two complementary colours – in this case yellow and blue – against the rich red, which gives the photo the depth that would otherwise be lacking.

The position of colours on this wheel give a clue as to how they will interact in an image. The simplest and most harmonious combinations are those of colours that are adjacent on the wheel. Just as they blend from one to another on the wheel (and, indeed, in a rainbow spectrum), so they seem to be a part of a close sequence in a photograph. This works in most examples, but there are exceptions to this. Very strong colours just a little distance apart on the wheel can clash – for example, a bright red against a bright magenta. In reality, the colour wheel should be a continuous progression of colours, and it is only for convenience that it is usually shown divided into segments. A sharp jump across a segment, without the muting effect of atmosphere or dilution, can cause a clash.

Any image that contains more than one hue automatically has within it colour relationships. We saw earlier how certain proportions of opposed colours created a particular kind of harmony, but in contrast to this, a small spot of colour creates another kind of colour energy. The relationship between the hues is then less important than the great difference in the size of the coloured areas in the frame.

One of the most obvious and useful ways of using a colour accent is in a landscape or setting that is drab and lacks colour. Many urban and industrial views, particularly under cloudy skies, have this appearance. A single spot of colour – from a brightly-clothed passer-by or a bunch of flowers, for instance – will enliven the photograph.

BELOW AND OPPOSITE BOTTOM RIGHT Two scenes that would most probably not warrant a second look if it were not for the simple addition of a small burst of colour. With these examples, the photographer adjusted the composition of the photo to accommodate the colour accent.

92

LEFT In this shot of the 'Blackbird' aircraft, orange and blue are used to bold advantage.

ABOVE Here, three subjects have been employed to draw the eye from the drab grey-green of the rest of the scene; the red bucket, the washing hanging up, and the bundle of clothes to the right. They interact to draw the eye from left to right.

Whereas the overall drabness of the setting might provide no focus of attention, and even discourage you from taking a photograph, a bright colour accent will change the whole structure of the view. It attracts attention and provides a visual counterpoint to its surroundings.

Any essentially monochrome view has the potential for using a colour accent. Other scenes that have a uniformity of hue include snow-blanketed landscapes and long-distance shots of rolling green fields. Photographed like this, they may well have a monochromatic beauty that stands well alone. There may, in other words, be good reasons for not attempting to add a spot of colour. If, however, you do include a colour accent, it will change the nature of the image considerably. Warm, bright colours are usually the most effective – splashes of red, orange or yellow. Nevertheless, beware of cliches: for example, a red-jacketed figure in a landscape has been over-used.

The colour psychology involved in this type of composition is such that the colour accent often works best when very small. By occupying a tiny part of the frame, it becomes unexpected, and fights for attention more strongly than if it were larger.

Bear this in mind when choosing a camera position and selecting the focal length of lens – a wide-angle lens may be more suitable because it takes in a broader panorama.

Colour can also play a very different role in a photograph – bringing a touch of strangeness to the image. Filters are probably the most obvious method, but the choice of film can also make a surprising difference.

The simplest way of doing this is to use a strongly coloured filter in a single hue. At a stroke, this changes the nature of the image, and there are no restrictions to the choice. The correction and balancing filters that we looked at earlier offer only a modest change, but those intended mainly for altering the response of black-and-white film are much more intense. These range from primaries like red (25 in Kodak's Wratten series of gelatin filters), to more exotic hues such as the strong pink of a Wratten 32. An alternative that offers more control and greater possibilities for manipulation is a coloured graduated filter. In this design, only half of the filter is tinted, and the edge of the tint is soft, so that in use there is no hard visible edge to the colour. A typical application for graduated filters is

ABOVE The dash of green in this shot is relatively unimportant if looked at in terms of its size in the frame, and yet the photograph would be lost without it. Imagine the picture without the small flash of colour; the blue would look bland and lifeless.

RIGHT The strange mauve cast in this landscape is the result of the use of Kodak Infrared Ektachrome film, which is partly sensitive to infra-red wavelengths. Infra-red sensitivity can make exposure calculations a little tricky, so it is advisable to bracket.

95

for the addition of colour to the sky, with the colour fading away at the horizon.

The danger in making this kind of colour manipulation is that it is almost too easy to do, and as a result can be a meaningless exercise. After experimenting with a few filters to see the possibilities, it is important to discriminate in the photographs you apply it to. Always think first whether the image would be better treated normally. If you set up a slide duplicating system you may find that it gives you greater freedom to play with different colour treatments if you add coloured filters only when making copies of slides, not when shooting originals. When making prints, add the filters during enlargement, for the same reason.

One special type of film automatically gives a transposition of the normal colours in a scene. Infra-red Ektachrome is a 'false-colour' film that is partly sensitive to infra-red wavelengths, and has its three dye layers arranged unrealistically. While scientific uses are its main application, its pictorial effect is unusual enough to justify experimenting. Exposure calculations are a little difficult to make, because of its infra-red sensitivity – ordinary exposure meters do not respond in the same way. It is best to bracket

exposures. The main drawback with this film is that it must be processed in the outdated E-4 process. Only a few distributors stock the appropriate chemicals for this; a list of their names are available from Kodak.

One of the special qualities of colour is that it can easily create a very subjective and emotional response. It is this that sets it apart in type from other graphic qualities such as shape, line, form and texture. They are all qualities that define an image, but colour goes further than this. The hue, or combination of hues, has particular associations for different people, and these can sometimes be very strong.

The reasons that underlie our often complex reactions to colours are a mixture of physiology and psychology, and the two are not always easy to separate. The physiological responses depend very much on the way our eyes and visual cortex operate. Of all wavelengths, the human eye is most sensitive to yellow-green (hence the tint of pilot's glasses). Because of this, yellow seems to us to be vibrant and active, while the hues to which the eye responds less well, such as blues and violets, seem more passive and quieter.

PROCESSING BLACK & WHITE

6

DEVELOPING THE FILM

■ BASIC TECHNIQUE

Processing black-and-white film is one of the simplest procedures in photography, and certainly easier and quicker than processing colour materials. There are five stages involved: developing, stop bath, fixing, washing and drying. By the time the processing is about to begin, the film has been exposed, and carries what is known as a 'latent' image. Those silver halide crystals that have been struck by light have undergone a very small reaction that needs the help of a developing solution before it can be seen.

The developer acts on the exposed crystals, and converts them into metallic silver, which is black and stable. The timing controls the quantity of black silver, and if the film were left in the developer too long, the image would eventually be obliterated. So, once the developer has acted for long enough, it is poured away and replaced with a stop bath.

This completely halts any more development, and is a good idea because, even with the tank freshly emptied, drops of developer remain on the emulsion. Following this, the fixing solution dissolves away the remaining unexposed silver halide crystals. Washing removes all traces of fixer and the dissolved halides, and must be thorough, or else the image that the negative carries will not stay permanent.

For equipment and materials, look back to the earlier section of this book. In addition to these basic items, you will need the following chemical solutions: developer; stop bath; fixer; and a recommended optional extra – wetting agent. Of these, there is an important choice only in the developer. Several manufacturers produce solutions that are essentially similar in action, and the most convenient choice is usually the one recommended in the instruction leaflet packed with the film.

Developers are supplied in powder or liquid concentrates, and must be mixed and diluted before

BELOW Certain basic precautions can, if taken, make the difference between success and disaster. These include using clean graduates, mixing powdered chemicals thoroughly and ensuring correct solution strength. When loading film, check the drum lid is secure to prevent light leaks, and that the film is not buckled when being loaded.

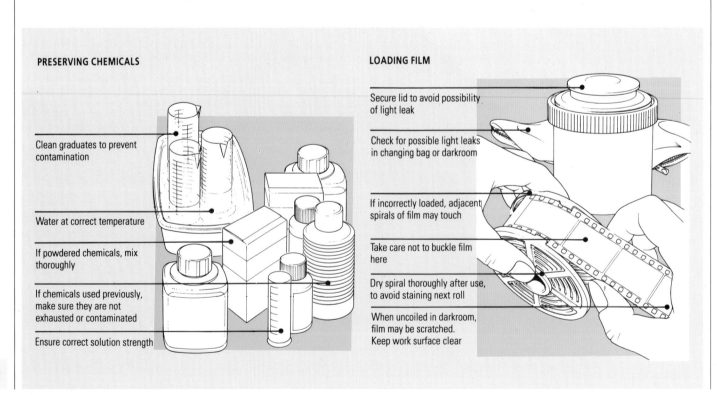

PRESERVING CHEMICALS

Clean graduates to prevent contamination

Water at correct temperature

If powdered chemicals, mix thoroughly

If chemicals used previously, make sure they are not exhausted or contaminated

Ensure correct solution strength

LOADING FILM

Secure lid to avoid possibility of light leak

Check for possible light leaks in changing bag or darkroom

If incorrectly loaded, adjacent spirals of film may touch

Take care not to buckle film here

Dry spiral thoroughly after use, to avoid staining next roll

When uncoiled in darkroom, film may be scratched. Keep work surface clear

RIGHT The production of a visible black-and-white image is a simple matter of realizing the 'latent' image already present on the exposed frame of film. This is achieved by immersing the film in developer, which acts on exposed silver halide crystals, converting them into metallic silver, which is black and stable.

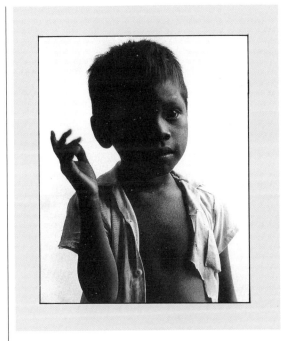

use. Normally, there are two alternative methods of use: to mix just enough for the number of films you intend to develop, discarding the used developer each time; or making up a larger quantity and re-using it. If you re-use developer, the time must be increased progressively. For instance, with Kodak's D-76, a typical standard developer, the first two uses can be performed at the recommended time, the next two for 6% longer, and the fifth and sixth for 12% longer. After that, throw the solution away. With this method, which saves money, you must keep a careful note on the storage bottle of how often it has been used.

■ BASIC PROCESSING

First of all, read the instructions that come with the developer very carefully. There are two important variables that are linked – the development time and the temperature – and the leaflet will show your choices. The normal temperature for black-and-white films is 20°C (68°F), but there is a range cooler and warmer than this that can be used, provided that you adjust the development time. Typically, for each 2 degrees C (3.6°F) cooler, add 10% to the time, and for each 2 degrees C warmer (3.6°F), develop for 10% less time. The workable temperature range is normally from about 18–24°C (64–75°F).

Plan the times from the point at which the tank has been filled to the point at which it has been drained. So, first practise pouring away a solution so that you know how long it will take.

Once you have filled the tank with developer, it needs to be agitated so that the solution acts evenly on all parts of the film. There are a number of techniques, but the most common is that shown, in which the tank is inverted (be sure that the cap is secure on the central filling hole and that you hold the tank in such a way that the lid cannot fall off). If you do not agitate enough, the emulsion will be developed unevenly, but there will be a different type of unevenness, called surge marks, if there is too much agitation.

In place of the stop bath (a mild solution of acetic acid), you could use plain water, although this does not halt the development as quickly. Both this and the fixer can be re-used several times. If it is important to complete the processing quickly, two other things will help. One is a rapid fixer instead of the normal version; the other is a clearing agent called hypo eliminator, which is used after the fix to reduce washing time from 30 to five minutes.

1 First mix the developer to the required dilution, and bring it to 20°C/68°F (or another recommended temperature) by placing the graduated jug in a deep dish of warm water.
2 Pour the developer into the tank. Start the time.
3 Smartly tap the tank on a hard surface to dislodge any air bubbles.
4 Agitate the tank as recommended.
5 Pour away the developer about 10 seconds before the end of time – or at least, so that the timer finishes just as the tank is emptied.
6 Pour in stop bath or water. Agitate as recommended.
7 Return the stop bath to its container at the end of the set time.
8 Pour in fixer and agitate as recommended.
9 Return the fixer to its bottle for further use.
10 Remove the tank's lid and wash the film by inserting a short length of hose into the core of the reel.
11 When the wash is complete, add a few drops of wetting agent. This checks the risk of drying marks.
12 Attach a film clip to the exposed end of the film, and pull out from its reel.
13 Hang the film on a clothes line, weighting the lower end with a second clip. Run a wetted sponge or squeegee down the strip to remove drops of water.

BLACK-AND-WHITE FILM PROCESSING PROCEDURE

Before beginning black-and-white processing, there are a number of important points to remember. Firstly, it is important that all chemicals are fresh. Secondly, ensure that your darkroom is completely light-proof; too many films are ruined by light leaks. Lastly, ensure that the film is well agitated in the developer solution.

1. In complete darkness, open the cassette by prising off the end with a bottle opener or special cassette opener. Take out the film and cut off the tongue

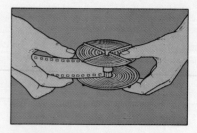

2. Holding the film by its edges, bow it carefully and attach to the spike or clip at the core of the reel. Rotate the reel so that the film is pulled out along the grooves and thread inwards from rim.

3. Trim off the end of the film that was attached to the cassette spool, lower the loaded reel into the developer tank and replace the lid. The room light can now be switched on.

4. Having checked the temperature of the developer solution, pour it quickly into the tank. When full, tap the tank to dislodge air bubbles, and fit the cap that covers the lid's central opening.

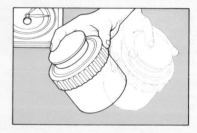

5. Trip the timer switch. During development agitate the tank by rocking it backwards and forwards to ensure even application of the solution. Agitate for 15 seconds every minute.

6. At the end of the development time, quickly pour out the developer. Pour in stop bath and agitate continuously for 30 seconds. Pour out and re-fill with fixer for the time recommended by the manufacturer.

7. When the fixing period is over, empty the tank, take off the lid and insert a hose from the cold water tap into the core of the reel. Wash for at least 30 minutes in gently running water. Strong water pressure may damage the emulsion.

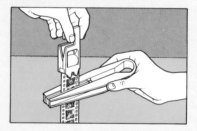

8. Remove the reel from the tank and attach film clips to both ends before hanging up in a dust-free atmosphere to dry. Tongs should be used with care as they can easily scratch film.

ASSESSING THE NEGATIVE

Faults apart, an assessment of the density and contrast of the negative will help in planning the print, which we deal with on the following pages. Experience in looking at many different negatives, and then printing them, will show what standard density and normal contrast are. For now, one simple guide to density is to press the negative flat down on a sheet of printed white paper, such as the page of a book. If the exposure and development have been normal, the lettering should just be visible through the darkest areas in the negative. In order to be able to make a proper assessment of a negative, you must be in a position to study it closely and with efficient back-lighting. The ideal equipment is a light box and a loupe; proprietary light boxes use fluorescent strip-lights backed with white reflecting metal or plastic, covered with a sheet of translucent plastic. They are relatively expensive, but it is fairly straightforward to build your own. The important criterion is that the illumination is even, yet bright.

Not even a home-made light box is entirely necessary. A plain white sheet of paper illuminated by an ordinary desk lamp aimed downwards is effective and simple; if you then support a plain sheet of glass over this (on two piles of books, for instance), the negative strip can be laid flat for close examination with a loupe.

Faults can occur in three areas of the photography, and it is important to identify which applies to a particular error. The three areas are: the condition of the film; the exposure; and the processing. The first of these is the least likely, but includes manufacturing defects and bad storage. While photographers, and even some camera manufacturers, are ready to identify the film makers as the

EVALUATING THE NEGATIVE

In the first shot **1**, the meter has been misled by the bright highlight behind, and as a result, the negative is underexposed. There is more detail in **2**, and it would be much easier to print. **3** and **4** have a 2-stop exposure difference between them. Note how the piano player who is virtually invisible in **3**, appears when the exposure has been opened up. The metering has been misled by the small, brightly lit scene in the centre of **5**, resulting in overexposure. The photographer compensated in **6**, by stopping down, but underdevelopment has aggravated the problem, causing burned out highlights. Negative **7** has a heavy sky (it was blue) and would print flat white. The sky area in **8** would print much darker because the photographer had fitted a red filter to the lens.

Fogging in camera: opaque areas may be visible at the edges of the film, though the middle should be clear.

Scratching: parallel scratches indicate grit either on the film cassette mouth or in the squeegee used to dry the film.

Fogging: opaque areas that should be clean and clear, almost certainly due to light reaching the film while loading into the tank. All-over density throughout the film could also be fogging of a different sort. This could be the remains of silver halide still in the emulsion which has not been 'cleared' by fixing. A re-fix can cure the problem.
Underdeveloped strip: down one side of film, caused by insufficient developer in the tank. All the film must be immersed under the developer. If one film is developed in a two-spiral tank, it is possible for the single spiral to move upward during agitation. Use the securing device supplied with the tank.

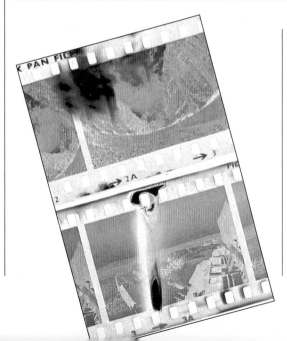

An ill-defined dark area is characteristic of accidental exposure to light. Here, this includes the rebate suggesting that the leak occurred outside the camera (left). Two adjacent pieces of the film stuck together in the reel in the developing tank, preventing full exposure to the processing solutions (bottom left).

culprits in many situations, the truth is that defects are very rare. More often than not, the cause of the fault lies in the camera, the way it is used, and in the darkroom.

The examples that follow are some of the most typical, and are intended to help you identify ones that you may come across. There are not many generalizations that are useful, but one is this: if the blemish, or whatever form the fault takes, extends beyond the rectangle of the picture frame, it has almost certainly not occurred during the exposure. The rebates themselves can offer quite a lot of information, particularly about the processing. These rebates carry printed frame numbers and the film's name, and as this has been pre-exposed by the manufacturer, it is consistent. In other words, if this lettering appears either weak or dense, it indicates an error in processing, rather than an exposure error.

Processing errors usually happen because the photographer was not paying full attention, or through inexperience. Always make an effort to find out exactly what happened – the only positive value of a mistake is that you can in future avoid doing the same thing.

Some faults can be cured or concealed, by re-touching, special treatment, or in the printing. Only throw away a damaged negative if you are absolutely sure that you can make nothing of it.

THE CONTACT SHEET

A contact sheet, also known as a proof sheet, is a print of several negatives made without enlargement and used as a visual reference. This is both a record of your black-and-white pictures and an aid to selecting a negative for making an enlargement. Normally, all the negatives from one roll of film are printed on a single contact sheet, and this is usually the first thing that is done after the film has been processed.

The equipment and materials are, more or less, those for normal printing. One extra item is a contact printing frame, or at least a sheet of glass for pressing down the negative strips onto the printing paper. An enlarger is not necessary for this stage but, as the point of making a contact sheet is to prepare for printing, you might as well use the enlarger as a light source.

First prepare the chemicals: developer, stop bath and fixer. If you intend to continue with a printing session, make sufficient quantities for a number of prints.

■ MAKING A CONTACT PRINT

Using a graduate, mix each solution in turn, washing the graduate throughly between mixings. The developer at least should be at 20°C; the stop bath and fixer can be between 18 and 24°C.

2 Fill three trays with the solutions to a depth of about ½in. Arrange them in order and, if you need the remainder, label them.

If necessary, clean with an airbrush the strip of negatives that you wish to make a contact sheet from.

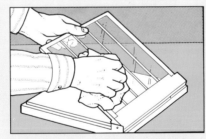
Ensure that the contact printing frame is free from dust and grit that may show on the contact sheet.

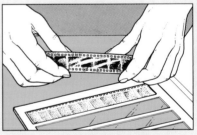
Arrange the clean strips of negatives in the printing frame, emulsion side down.

Adjust the enlarger so that, with no negative in the carrier and de-focused, it illuminates an area large enough to cover the printing frame.

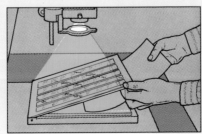
Ensure that your printing paper is placed emulsion side up on the base of the contact printing frame.

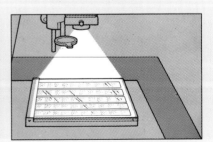
Close the frame and place it on the enlarger's baseboard. Make the exposure, and remember that here it may be necessary to experiment.

3 Turn the safelight on and the room light off. Wash and dry your hands.

4 Adjust the enlarger so that, with no negative in the carrier and de-focused, it illuminates an area large enough to cover the contact printing frame.

5 Remove one sheet of paper from its box and place it, emulsion side up, on the base of the contact printing frame. Arrange the negative strips on top, emulsion side down.

6 Close the frame, and place it on the enlarger's baseboard. Make the exposure (you will need to experiment with this the first time).

7 Remove the paper, slide it into the developer, and rock the tray gently for one minute.

8 Using tongs, take the paper out of the developer, drain it for a few seconds and slide it into the stop bath. Rock the tray for several seconds.

9 Remove and drain, then slide into the fixer. Agitate repeatedly for about two minutes. You can turn the room light on after 30sec.

10 Remove and wash in running water for about four minutes, with the water at the same temperature as the previous solutions.

11 Dry on a flat surface, having wiped off excess moisture with a squeegee.

BELOW Trying to find the best shot from a sequence in negative form can be – to say the least – tricky, and this is where the contact sheet comes into its own. Once the choice has been made, the negative can be singled out on the sheet by marking it with a soft, erasable pencil such as a chinagraph.

RIGHT The very fact that a contact sheet image is so small means that any mistakes during the printing or processing will make the picture virtually unviewable. Always ensure that your chemicals are fresh, and that the sheet is thoroughly washed.

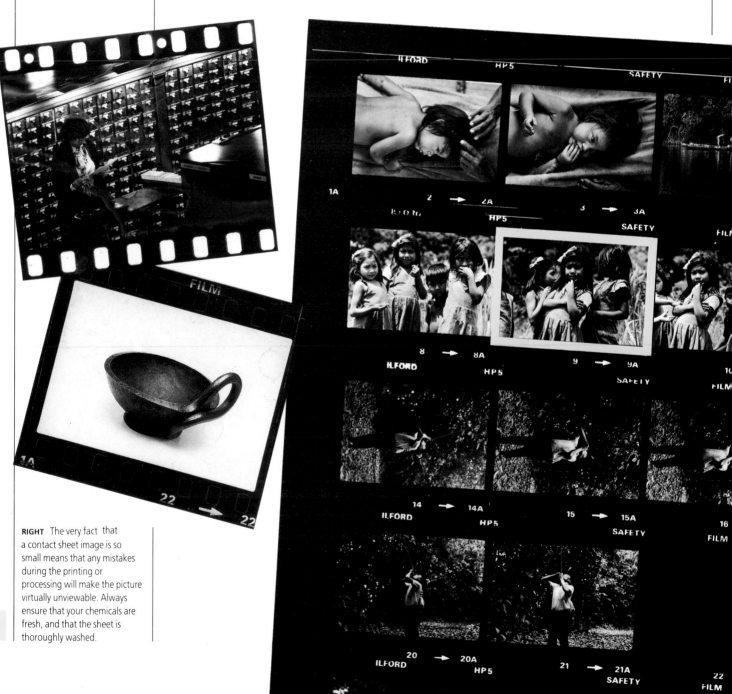

ABOVE Contact sheets are both easy to produce and provide a quick means for assessing your negatives. To make the most of the sheets, however, it is wise to invest in a magnifier of some description.

MAKING A TEST PRINT

With the negative and contact sheet at hand, you are ready to select one frame for printing. Once you have chosen the negative, the cropping and the size of the enlargement, the next stage is to find the best overall exposure.

The processing stages are the same as for the contact sheet, except that some photographers like to vary the development time according to how the image comes up. To begin with, however, it is best to stick to a standard procedure: the fewer variables, the easier it is to make adjustments. In any case, prepare all the chemicals as shown on the previous pages.

1 Prepare the developer, stop bath and fixer to the point of having an ordered row of trays, all at the right temperature.

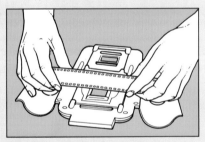

Place the negative in the enlarger's negative carrier (emulsion side down), cleaning off any dust with a blower, anti-static brush or anti-static gun.

Insert the carrier in the enlarger head. With the room lights out, the enlarger head on and the lens aperture wide open, adjust the enlarger head until the image is focused and the size you have chosen.

Adjust the focus until the image is critically sharp. This can be judged either by eye alone or with the use of a grain magnifier.

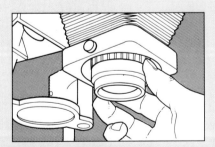

Close down the lens aperture about two stops (normally this would be f11). With a negative of normal density, this will let you use reasonably short exposure times, and the lens performance will be at its peak. Greater depth of field will also compensate for any focusing errors.

Under safelight illumination, and with the enlarger lamp off, insert a sheet of normal (Grade 2) paper, emulsion side up, into the printing frame and set the timer to 5 seconds.

Hold a piece of black card over the sheet of paper, leaving just a quarter of its width exposed, and give a 5-second exposure. Move the card along for a second exposure of 5 seconds. Make third and fourth exposures in the same way.

BELOW A standard series of exposure times, from five to twenty seconds, gives a good indication of what the final exposure should be. From the examination of the negative, the central part of the picture with its range of skin tones is the most important, and the test bands were arranged so that the most likely exposure falls in this area. Twenty-second and fifteen-second exposures are too dark, with obvious loss of detail in shadow areas, while five seconds leaves the highlights white and featureless. The ten second exposure is almost right, but perhaps a little too dark.

20sec/f11   15sec/f11   10sec/f11   5sec/f11

RIGHT Choose from the negative the most important tones and try and cover these with each exposure.

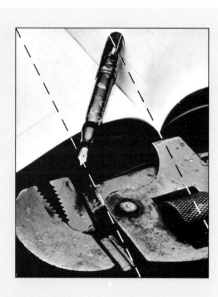

2 Take the negative strip, hold it by its edges, and place it, emulsion side down, in the enlarger's negative carrier.

3 Remove dust from the negative with a burst of compressed air or a soft anti-static brush. Hold it at an angle under the enlarger's light for a close check.

4 Place a sheet of plain white paper, such as the back of a discarded print, in the easel, and adjust the easel's masks to approximately the proportions that you want. This paper will make composition faster and focusing easier.

5 Turn the safelight on and the room light off. With the lens at full aperture, adjust the enlarger head so that the image fills the frame and is sharply focused.

6 Make final adjustments to the easel masks, as necessary.

7 Reduce the lens aperture by about two stops from fully open. On most lenses this gives the best optical performance.

8 Take a fresh sheet of printing paper and insert it in the easel, emulsion side up, replacing the plain white sheet.

9 Cover all of the exposed paper except for a narrow strip (about 20% of the area) with a piece of thick, opaque card. Make a 5sec exposure.

10 Move the card to uncover a little more of the paper, and give another 5sec exposure. Continue this until all the paper has been exposed (for the last exposure the sheet should be completely uncovered).

11 Process the paper as described earlier, for one minute in the developer, several seconds in the stop bath, and in the fixer for two minutes.

12 Wash and dry.

CHOOSING THE PAPER

Interestingly, printing papers are available in a wider range of characteristics than black-and-white film. Apart from size, printing papers come in different paper thicknesses, textures, tints, tones, types of coating and, probably, most important of all, contrast grades. Speed, however, is not offered as a variable, but the way in which it is used renders such a choice unimportant. There is no difficulty in altering the exposure by almost any degree, unlike many camera situations. In order to allow workable exposure times of at least a few seconds, paper sensitivity to light is less than that of film.

CONTRAST GRADE

To compensate for low or high contrast in the negative, paper is available in several grades of contrast. The normal grade is 2, low-contrast is 1 (for contrasty negatives), and high-contrast grades are 3 and 4 (for flat negatives). This is the basic range, but some paper manufacturers produce a 0 grade – extremely low contrast – and a 5 grade, which is very high, or 'hard'.

An alternative is variable-contrast paper – a single type that will give a range depending on whether a bluish or yellowish filter is used in the enlarger. The advantage of this is that you need only buy one stock of paper.

WEIGHT

This is a measure of paper thickness. The most commonly available are single weight and double weight, the latter being better for significant enlargement because it has less tendency to crease or buckle.

TEXTURE

This refers to both the smoothness of the surface and to textural patterns introduced for special effect. The smoother the surface, the less scattering of light there is, and the deeper the blacks. So, for a good range of contrast and rich shadow tones, glossy paper is for many photographers the ideal. Except for resin-coated (RC) paper, this can be 'ferrotyped' by drying it in contact with a smooth metal plate to give an even glossier effect, but an unglazed finish is more usual. Common alternatives to glossy are matte, lustre and pearl.

In addition, special papers are made to imitate the surface of an oil canvas, silk, and so on.

TINT

White paper is normal, giving the most brilliance in highlights, but slightly tinted stock, such as cream, is also available.

TONE

The mixture of chemicals in the emulsion determines the exact tone of the dark parts of the image, which can tend towards blue-black, brown-black, warm-black, or may just be neutral.

COATING

An alternative to standard, paper-base paper, and one that is becoming increasingly popular, is resin-coating. These papers have a water-resistant base that confines the processing chemicals to the emulsion and speeds up the fixing, washing and drying.

LEFT While it is almost impossible to illustrate different paper finishes in print, the examples shown here may give some idea how great a difference the paper and finish can make to the final result, when development is the same for each print. One of the most obvious effects is the scattering of light on a textured surface (such as the linen bases shown here) which results in shallower blacks. For rich shadow tones, glossy papers are therefore preferred.

LEFT , FROM RIGHT TO LEFT
Resin-coated glossy; Kentmere textured matt; Ilford Galerie; (middle) fibre-based glossy, unglazed; tinted linen base; white linen; (bottom) Chlorobromide fibre-based, matt; fibre-based glossy, unglazed; Chlorobromide fibre-based glossy, unglazed.

THE FINAL PRINT

With the test print complete, you can now evaluate it and choose the settings for the final print. Study the different exposures – the palest received 5sec, the next 10sec, and so on. Decide which looks best, and set the enlarger time to this. Also check the test print for dust marks, and if necessary clean the negative again (but do not simply blow air into the enlarger head; that will throw up hidden dust).

At this point you may also decide that some changes are needed to the overall contrast and to local density. Contrast changes are made by choosing a different grade (or a different filter if you are using variable-contrast paper), but there may be a difference in speed between them. If you change from grade 2 to grade 3, for example, the print may need less exposure. The difference will not be great, so it may be sufficient to take a small cut piece of paper and make a single exposure as a test.

If some areas of the print seem to need more or less exposure, you will need to use some of the print controls described earlier. Even so, until you have the experience to be able to predict the exact amount of shading and burning-in, it will probably be easier to make one straight, unmanipulated first print. Then you can examine this to calculate variations in exposure for a later print.

NEGATIVE CARRIERS

Glassless negative carriers (above) are quite adequate for 35mm film but larger formats need glass (right) to hold them flat.

■ MAKING THE FINAL PRINT

1 Prepare the chemicals as before (although normally, this stage of final printing follows the test print).
2 With the safelight on and the room light off, check the composition and focus once more – particularly if you have removed the negative carrier to remove any more dust.
3 Remove a sheet of paper from its box and insert it in the easel.
4 Make the exposure to the chosen time.
5 Process the paper as before.

LEFT The final print.

THE FINAL PRINT – PROCEDURE

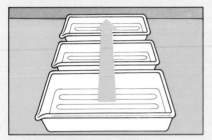

1 Check that the three chemicals – developer, stop bath and fixer – are in the right order, and that the developer is at 20°C (68°F). Make the exposure.

2 Slide the paper, emulsion side down, into the developer tray. Press it down with the developer tongs so that it is fully immersed.

3 Turn the paper over so that the emulsion side is facing up and you can see the developing image.

5 Lift the paper out of the developer tray with the tongs and allow excess solution to drip off. Transfer the paper to the stop bath, take care not to dip the developer tongs into the stop bath. Rock the tray as during development.

6 After 10secs, lift the print out of the stop bath and drain. Transfer to the fixer, rocking the tray at intervals. After one or two minutes, you can switch on the room lights and examine the print. Leave it in the fixer for at least 10 mins, but no more than 20 mins

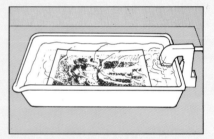

7 Wash the print in running water to remove all traces of the chemicals; washing time varies according to paper manufacturer's recommendations. If the paper is resin-coated, it needs washing for only 4 mins; paper-based papers need about 15 mins.

DRYING THE PRINT

Resin-coated prints Dry them flat without using a dryer. Air-drying print racks are ideal, as water cannot get trapped underneath the prints. Resin-coated prints can be dried back-to-back, pegged on a clothes line over a bath.

Paper-based prints These should be dried in a heated dryer (a flatbed machine is normal). Glossy prints can be glazed by being placed face down on the dryer's metal plate. The majority of professional photographers use glossy paper unglazed (ie dried face up).

4 Agitate the solution by rocking the tray gently. This ensures that the paper receives even development. Develop for 90 seconds.

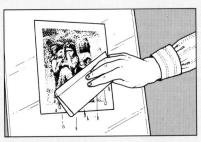

8 Put the print against a smooth, flat surface, and wipe off water drops.

EMBELLISHING THE PRINT

The usual answer to high contrast, where the range of tones in the negative is beyond that of the print, is to change to a lower contrast grade of paper. This, however, affects the entire image, whereas often it is only local areas that need help. For instance, on an overcast day, in a landscape composed so that there is just a small area of sky, the brightness range below the horizon is likely to be fairly limited. So, for this principal part of the image, a contrast grade of 3, or even 4, would do well, yet the sky would come out a blank white in a straightforward print. Changing to a softer grade of paper would bring the sky within the range of the print's tonal range, but at the serious cost of dullness elsewhere.

Another typical situation which causes uneven brightness across an image is an on-camera flash picture. Because of the position of the flash unit, nearer objects will be brighter than those in the background. If you have not already composed the photograph to take care of this, you will be left with a negative which, if printed normally, has too great a range of tones.

The solution to these and similar problems is to give selected areas of the print more or less exposure than normal, by moving your hands or a shaped piece of card in the path of light from the enlarger lens. Holding back the light from an area is called

SHADING-IN TECHNIQUE

1 Your hand may be used to shade the print, although keep it moving to prevent sharp contrasts between affected and unaffected areas.

2 Shading tools are commercially available, these being designed to shade specific areas.

3 Cupped hands may be used to control the size of the area during printing in.

Despite their involving related techniques, blocking-out and burning-in produce dramatically different results, even with the same image. Burning-in (above) has given a sinister mood to the picture while dodging (right) has lightened the atmosphere.

ABOVE Printed straight, this picture sorely lacks impact; the sky is the main culprit, being as it is bleached and devoid of detail.

RIGHT However, a simple process of burning-in – selectively preventing light from reaching the print during exposure – restores sufficient contrast to the sky for the image to regain its punch.

dodging or shading; giving extra exposure is called burning-in or printing-in.

You can either make or buy printing tools. Dodging tools include large sheets of black card to cover big areas that run over an edge of the frame (such as the sky) and small discs, ovals and other shapes each attached to a length of wire for small areas inside the print (such as faces). The wires are necessary to avoid shading more than a limited area, and in use a dodging tool must be moved constantly, otherwise the shadow of the wire rod will print distinctly.

Tools for burning-in are basically large sheets of black card, each cut with a hole of a particular shape. Again in use they must be moved around all the time to keep the edge projected by the hole soft and indistinct on the print. For this same reason, it is easier to blend the effect of burning-in, or dodging, if the printing tool is held at a distance from the print – the further away it is, the more out of focus the edges will be. Thus, if you are making your own tools, it is often better to keep them fairly small, because raising the tool away from the print will cause it to cover a larger area on the print.

With burning-in, always use a sheet of black card large enough to cover a bigger area than the print; it is surprisingly easy when using this technique to be so absorbed in controlling the patch of light in the middle that you do not notice stray light at the edges of the print.

Rather than prepare several large sheets of black card for burning-in, an alternative is to make one with a fairly large central hole, and to stick over this one of a set of differently shaped apertures cut into smaller pieces of black paper.

Some darkroom workers prefer to use their hands rather than specially-prepared tools, although this method only works for burning-in and for shading from the edge of the print inwards. You cannot successfully shade an isolated area within the image by using your hand – your wrist will shade adjacent parts also. In addition, you should be particularly careful when burning-in to avoid light catching the edges of the print. Nevertheless, using hands for printing controls has an advantage in that the shape of the edge can be formed by contorting the fingers, and this edge can be softened by finger movements (almost like kneading dough).

Finally, for an edge that is convoluted but needs to be shaded precisely, you can cut around the image made on a test print to give an exact match.

Retouching is a skill that can be used both to correct faults and to introduce major changes and special effects. At its least noticeable and simplest, retouching is simply a matter of 'spotting': that is, using dyes on the tip of a fine paintbrush to clear up dust specks on a print. Most retouching, in fact, is confined to tidying up the image and correcting mistakes, although as a matter of principle it is better to avoid the faults in the first place by handling the film carefully at all stages, from exposure to processing.

The level of skill that you need depends partly on the medium. Prints are much easier to work on than film, and black-and-white is easier than colour. If you shoot in 35mm, detailed retouching is all but impossible, because of the size of the negative. The larger the form of the image, the better. If, however, there is something that can be done to the negative, this will later be much more convenient than retouching each individual print made from the same negative.

There are four possible retouching techniques, and while it is only rarely that all need to be used together on the same image, they should be applied in the following order:

1 Chemical baths (eg reducing or intensifying the negative, or bleaching areas of the print).
2 Dyes.
3 Knifing and any other physical attention.
4 Opaque pigment.

This order is important. For instance, if you add a dye over a part of the print that has already been knifed, it will run uncontrollably into the damaged area and seep under the surrounding emulsion.

In principle, plan the retouching beforehand, starting on broad areas and finishing with the finest details. With every technique, do a little at a time, building up the effect slowly. One of the most common mistakes in retouching is to overdo it.

■ EQUIPMENT AND MATERIALS

For retouching a print, work on a well-lit surface: an adjustable desk-lamp is ideal. For bleaching, have a dilute solution, cotton swabs, and plenty of water available nearby to halt the bleaching effect. Sets of transparent dyes in a range of off-blacks make it possible to mix one that matches the print image exactly. Use fine camel-hair brushes, a mixing palette and water for dilution. A scalpel or razor blade is for scraping away the top layer of the print emulsion, and opaque pigments in black-and-white

HOW TO RETOUCH PRINTS

Reducing print density:

1 Pre-soak the print in water for 10 minutes to soften the emulsion and paper-base.

2 Lay the print on a smooth surface, such as a sheet of glass, and swab off excess water.

3 With brushes or cotton swabs, apply the diluted bleach or reducing solution to the print. If you are in any doubt about how fast the solution will work, or whether it will cause any discolouration, test first on an unwanted print. In any case, use a very diluted solution so that you have more control. Work the solution over the print continuously so as to avoid hard and conspicuous edges to the reduced area.

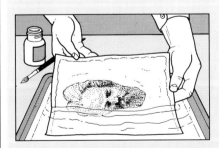

4 Use a cotton swab and either plain water or hypo to halt the bleaching action when you judge the effect to be right.

PAINTING WITH DYES

1 Pre-soak the print in water for 10 minutes. This enables the dye to penetrate more easily, and prevents hard edges to the dye washes.
2 On a sheet of glass, or other smooth working surface, swab off water droplets and allow the print to dry slightly for about 10 minutes.
3 With either rubber cement or self-adhesive masking film, mask off the areas that are to be untreated. Using a sharp scalpel, cut round the edges of the area to be dyed with just enough pressure to break the film but not enough to damage the print. Peel off the film from the areas that have been cut round. Mix a dilute

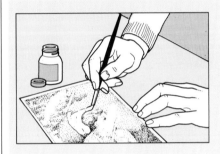

solution of dye, making sure that it matches the hue of the print. Working from two dye bottles, one brownish-black and other bluish-black, you can prepare a precise match. Apply the dye in washes with a brush. Build up the density in a number of applications. If you make a mistake, or find that the added density is too great, place the entire print under running water for several minutes and begin again.

KNIFING TO REMOVE DARK SPOTS

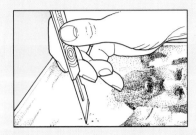

1 With the broad edge of a sharp scalpel blade, gently shave the blemish on the print's surface. Make short strokes, keeping your fingers steady and using your wrist for movement.
2 Stop before all the emulsion is removed, otherwise the roughened paper base will begin to show through.

3 For small spots, use the top of the blade, but remember that there is a greater risk with this method of cutting through to the paper base. Knifing should never be done before any wet retouching (such as bleaching or dye application) as it physically damages the print and can result in dye bleeding away from its area of application.

can be used (sparingly) to block out small details.

If the retouching has been so extensive that it shows in the altered surface of the print, it may be worth copying the print onto a fresh negative and then reprinting from that.

■ TONING

Although different makes of printing paper offer a subtle choice of colour shades in variations of black, a chemical toning solution gives a much bigger range. The most commonly used toner is sepia, but others include selenium, gold and multi-toners (which use a selection of colour couplers and a colour developer). Each has different procedures for use, and you should therefore study the manufacturer's instructions carefully. Because toners reduce the maximum density from the original black silver, toning procedures work most successfully on prints that have been exposed and developed quite heavily.

Sepia toning, the most common method of all, is a two-part or three-part process, depending on the final effect that you are looking for. In the first stage, soak the fixed and washed print in the bleach solution provided. You can do this by inspection, for a few minutes, until the image has faded to a pale yellowish-brownish colour. Then transfer the print to the toning solution, which will restore the image in sepia. For a richer brown image, give an additional soaking in the toner for two or three minutes before the bleach bath. For different effects, it is possible to apply either the bleach or both the bleach and toner locally, using a cotton swab.

Gold toning is a single solution, one-stage process. More than most toning procedures, its effect depends heavily on the type of print emulsion and on other treatments already used. It works progressively, up to about 20min, and it takes this full time for a regular silver-bromide paper to show a change towards blue-black. Chlorobromide paper, on the other hand, turns orange-brown, while a print that has first been sepia toned will turn out purple-brown after a few minutes or orange-red if given the full soaking.

RETOUCHING EQUIPMENT

Basic items are a can of compressed air (**1**), and an airbrush (**2**), with transparent masking film to cover areas not being retouched (**3**). Retouching fluid (**4**), gives a 'bite' to the print surface. Bleach (**5**) and hypo crystals (**6**) are also needed, and rubber cement (**7**) can be used for complicated masking. Watercolour pigments (**8**) are used in the airbrush and a scalpel (**9**) for cutting and knifing.

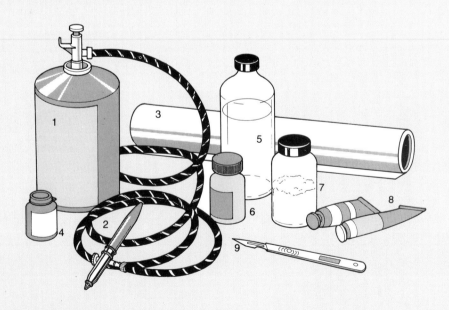

ABOVE AND BELOW Compare the blue-black bias in a gold toned print (below) with an untreated print featuring the same image (above).

ABOVE Sepia toning remains a popular technique, giving treated prints that brownish 'aged' look.

7

PROCESSING COLOUR

Look back to the recommended equipment section. First make sure that the colour negative film you have shot matches the processing kit; the majority of colour negative films are compatible with Kodak's C-41 process. The names of processing kits also vary, so check the packed information. The example used here is the Kodak Flexicolor Kit, which contains one pint of each solution except the developer, of which there are two pints. The solutions are in the form of liquid concentrates and powder.

First prepare the solutions according to the instructions. With those chemicals that are supplied in two parts, mix each part one at a time, not both together. Once prepared, the solutions should be stored in tightly stoppered bottles. The life of most solutions is about six or eight weeks, so mix them only when you need them.

Load the film, in darkness, onto the spiral reel. Make sure that the reel is the right width for the film you are using or, if it is an adjustable plastic reel, that it is set to the proper width (twist the two halves and then lock them into position). With a stainless steel reel, clip the end of the film onto the core of the reel, then turn the reel in one hand while pressing the sides of the film in gently with the other, so that the film feeds into the grooves from the inside outwards. With a plastic reel, push the film onto the grooves from the outside, so that it slides inwards to the centre. When the film has been loaded, place the reel inside the tank and replace the lid securely.

Next bring the solutions to working temperature. For the developer at least, this must be very accurately maintained, at 37.8°C (100°F) with no more than a 0.15°C (0.4°F) variation. The other solutions can be between 24 and 40.5°C (75 and 105°F), so it is usually easiest to warm everything to the temperature of the developer. The simplest method is to fill a deep tray with warm water and place the solution containers in this. It will take a short time (about 10 minutes) for the solutions to reach the right temperature, so that the bath should start a degree or two warmer than 37.8°C. Keep a constant eye on the thermometer, and stir the developer as it warms up.

Each of the processing steps requires a similar procedure: pouring the solution into the tank, starting the timer, agitating the tank, and finally pouring the solution away (either down the sink or back into its storage bottle, depending on the solution). Develop a consistent way of doing all this, so that the results are predictable and repeatable. For instance, start the timer when you have just finished pouring the solution in, and begin draining it away so that the last drop leaves the tank as the timer stops. If in doubt, practise with an empty tank and plain water. It should take about 10 seconds to drain out the liquid. Also, each time you pour a new solution into the tank, make a habit of tapping the whole tank against a hard surface to dislodge any air bubbles that might have

PROCESSING

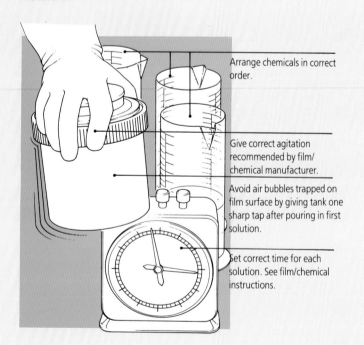

Arrange chemicals in correct order.

Give correct agitation recommended by film/chemical manufacturer.

Avoid air bubbles trapped on film surface by giving tank one sharp tap after pouring in first solution.

Set correct time for each solution. See film/chemical instructions.

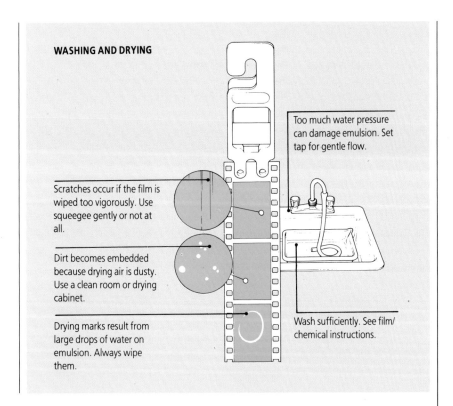

WASHING AND DRYING

Too much water pressure can damage emulsion. Set tap for gentle flow.

Scratches occur if the film is wiped too vigorously. Use squeegee gently or not at all.

Dirt becomes embedded because drying air is dusty. Use a clean room or drying cabinet.

Drying marks result from large drops of water on emulsion. Always wipe them.

Wash sufficiently. See film/chemical instructions.

become trapped on the film; this is particularly important with the developer, as it is being poured onto dry film.

Agitation is essential, and it must be done in a certain way to make sure that the film is acted on evenly, especially with the developer. There are two principal ways: inverting the tank or sliding it in a pattern on the worktop. Follow the diagram instructions, and if you invert it (the normal method), be sure to hold the lid and cap tightly to prevent spillage. Do not agitate continuously, but follow the sequence shown in the table.

After the developer, add the bleach. The temperature is less critical for this solution, but the film must still be in complete darkness. After the bleach, the other steps can be done in normal room lighting, but as you will still need to agitate the tank, it is usually more convenient to keep the lid on the tank. However, if you are eager to check the results, you can examine a few frames of the film about halfway into the fixing step.

After the final wash and stabilizer, attach a film clip to the end of the film, draw the entire length of film out from the reel, and hang it up to dry (a clothes line is convenient). Weight the bottom end of the film with a second clip and draw a squeegee or soft sponge, dipped in wetting agent, down the film from top to bottom. This action avoids spots and drying marks. Dry for at least 20 minutes in a dust-free room.

PROCESSING STEP	MINUTES*	°F	°C	AGITATION (SECONDS)		
PROCESSING KODACOLOR II AND KODACOLOR 400 FILMS IN THE KODAK FLEXICOLOR PROCESS KIT FOR PROCESS C-41 1 US Pint/473 ml/16 fl oz Size						
				INITIAL	REST	AGITATION
1 Developer	3¼	100±¼	37.8±0.15	30	13	2
2 Bleach	6½	75–105	24–40.5	30	25	5
Remaining steps can be done in normal room light.						
3 Wash	3¼	75–105	24–40.5			
4 Fixer	6½	75–105	24–40.5	30	25	5
5 Wash	3¼	75–105	24–40.5			
6 Stabilizer	1½	75–105	24–40.5	30		
7 Drying	10–20	75–110	24–43.5			
Includes 10-second drain time in each step.						

DEVELOPING TRANSPARENCIES

Many of the processing methods are the same for slide film as for negatives, although there are more steps. The reason for the extra steps is that, part way through the processing sequence, the image must be reversed so that the result is a transparency rather than a negative. Once again, first make sure that the film you are using can be processed in the chemicals; the standard process is Kodak's E-6, which is the example that we use here. Load the film into its tank, mix and prepare the solutions in the same way as described for colour negative films.

There are two developers in this process, one used at the beginning, the other used after the reversal bath. Both need to be used at the same precise temperature as the developer for colour negatives 37.8°C (100°F). The tolerances are also very tight: 0.3°C (0.5°F) for the first developer, 1.1°C (2°F) for the second developer. The remaining solutions are less demanding, but must be used between 33.5 and 39°C (92 and 102°F). Control the temperature in the same way as for colour negatives, but be a little more careful in maintaining the temperature of the bath after you have added the first developer – remember that the second developer, a few steps later, must also be at exactly 37.8°C (100°F).

Follow the procedures already described for colour negatives, using the table shown here for timings and steps. At the end, as you hang the film up to dry, it will be slightly milky, but this will clear as it dries. Only judge the quality of the results when the film is completely dry. A hair dryer will speed up this part of the process, but be careful not to overheat the film; do not exceed 50°C (122°F) to avoid distortion.

PUSH-PROCESSING

You can use E-6 slide films at a higher speed than their normal rating, provided that you extend the development. This can be very useful in low-light conditions. Simply treat the film as if it had a higher ISO when you shoot, and make a note on the film cassette to give it extra development. For example, you can use Ektachrome 400 film as if it were ISO 800 and gain an extra stop. To achieve this extra 1-stop increase, add 2 minutes to the first developer time (continue the pattern of agitation for these extra 2 minutes). That is all there is to it. For a 2-stop increase, add 5½ minutes to the first developer. You will find there will be some increase in graininess and contrast, and a slight change in colour, but with a 1-stop increase these are not likely to be great.

PROCESSING KODAK EKTACHROME FILMS IN PROCESS E-6						
For 1 US Pint/473 ml/16 fl oz Processing Tanks						
PROCESSING STEP	MINUTES*	°F	°C	AGITATION (SECONDS)		
				INITIAL	REST	AGITATION
1 First Developer	7†	100 ± ½	37.8 ± 0.3	30	15	5
2 Wash	1	92–102	33.5–39	30	15	5
3 Wash	1	92–102	33.5–39	30	15	5
4 Reversal Bath	2	92–102	33.5–39	30	80	—
Remaining steps can be done in normal room light.						
5 Col. Developer	6	100 ± 2	37.8 ± 1.1	30	25	5
6 Conditioner	2	92–102	33.5–39	30	80	—
7 Bleach	7	92–102	33.5–39	30	25	5
8 Fixer	4	92–102	33.5–39	30	25	5
9 Wash (running water)	6	92–102	33.5–39	30	25	5
10 Stabilizer	1	92–102	33.5–39	30	20	—
11 Drying	10–20	75–120	24–49			

Includes time required to drain tank (usually about 10 seconds).

For initial films through a 1 pint (473 ml) set of solutions.

See instructions accompanying the kit for Process E-6 for development times of subsequent films through the same set of solutions.

When over-developing – 'push-processing' – or under-developing – known as 'cutting' – perhaps in an attempt to compensate for exposure error or high/low light levels at the time of the shoot, you will not always know by how much to over- or under-develop. As a test, it is possible to take a short length of film from the beginning of the roll. In the dark, cut off sufficient film to include two or three frames and develop this test clip normally. By 'sacrificing' the first frames of the roll like this, you can then decide whether to 'push' – as in the photograph below right – or 'cut' – as in the print bottom right. The main picture, taken with a 400mm telephoto lens (1/60sec, f16) was developed normally. The others were over- and under-developed by one stop respectively.

Compare the contrast in the photograph above, developed normally, with that in the examples below (400mm, 1/60sec, f16).

This photograph has been 'pushed', or overdeveloped by one stop.

This version has been 'cut', or under-developed by one stop.

121

ASSESSING RESULTS

Of the two types of film, negative and slide, the first is more difficult to judge. Slide film, once processed, carries its image as it should be seen, and can be assessed by using a light-box, projector or slide-viewer. In a colour negative, however, both the tones and the colours are reversed. In addition, a built-in orange mask is included by the manufacturer to improve print quality. This mask overlays everything.

A well-exposed colour negative looks rather denser than an equivalent black-and-white negative. If you view it through an orange filter (such as an 85B or similar), this will give a better idea of the tones. Nothing short of a print, however, will show what the colours will look like. One of the most common faults is under-exposure: others are fogging because of a light leak, stains due to chemical contamination, and scratches. Fogging appears as a dark area, and extends over the rebates (the perforated margins of 35mm film); it can occur during the loading of the tank, by failing to seal the tank's lid properly, or if the camera back is accidentally opened before the film has been completely re-wound. If you develop one film at a time, you may have some opportunity to correct mistakes after the first has been processed. With the C-41 process, if you know that the films have been under-exposed by one stop, increase the development time by one third. This is really an emergency procedure, as colour negative films are not designed to perform as well as slide films do when push-processed.

Mistakes in processing slide film are easier to spot. Look for over-exposure and under-exposure, but realize that this may have been a mistake during shooting. Strong colour casts are probably due to chemical contamination; just a drop or two of bleach or fixer in the developer will have disastrous results.

1 An example of underdeveloped film; the image is too dark. On a negative, it would appear to be too pale.

2 An example of overdeveloped film; the same pale image can be caused by overexposure when taking the shot. The film speed may have been too slow.

3 Gross under-exposure; the transparency would appear to be almost black, the negative almost transparent. This is probably caused by a faulty shutter rather than any error on the photographer's part.

4 Unexposed film; the negative would be transparent and the transparency black. The film may not have been through the camera if the film tongue was not attached securely to the spool. Or perhaps a very high shutter speed was used with flash.

LEFT A well-exposed negative looks rather denser than an equivalent black-and-white negative. Viewing the negative through an orange filter, such as an 85B, will give a better idea of tones.

BELOW Crimp marks show up as pinkish or bluish crescents on transparencies. These are most often caused by buckling the film before processing. Take care when separating the film from the spool and loading it into the developing tank.

TOP AND ABOVE A high-contrast scene such as this could be ruined completely by the common fault of print under-exposure; all detail in the foreground subject could easily be lost altogether.

ABOVE AND RIGHT Colour slide film is far more critical of exposure than colour negative film, a fact that must be remembered when assessing your prints from slides. Much of the time, slight under- or over-exposure may be the fault of the original transparency. However, stains and noticeable colour casts may well be due to chemical contamination; a mere drop or two of bleach or fixer in the developer will have disastrous consequences. One thing you can't do much about, however, is an image which is simply out-of-focus. This can be spotted if you look carefully at the slide.

MAKING THE PRINT EXPOSURE

Although the colour filtration and exposure times vary from process to process, the essentials of making a colour enlargement are fairly standard. At the start, it may take you several tries before you arrive close to the best filtrations and exposures; the light output and optical parts of enlargers differ. If you use a simple enlarger with a black-and-white head, place a UV-absorbing 2B or CP2B filter permanently under the light head and above the negative carrier.

The first step after processing the film is to select the negatives or slides for printing. With slides, a light-box is sufficient to judge a well-exposed frame, but with negatives, make a contact sheet. As well as giving you your first look at the images, it will serve as a filing reference for later printing. Set the enlarger head at a height that will illuminate an area slightly larger than a 8×10-in (20× 26-cm) sheet of paper with the negative carrier empty. Judging the exposure and filtration is something of a chicken-and-egg situation, because you must first have some experience with the enlarger and negative/paper combination that you regularly use. After you have set up your system for the first time, this will be no problem; for now, assume that you have calibrated everything. Set the filtration, aperture and timer according to previous test prints. Place one film, cut into strips of six frames each, in a contact-printer or under a plain sheet of glass. In safelighting, place a sheet of printing paper underneath and expose.

Having selected a negative or slide to print, place it in the negative carrier with the emulsion side down, facing the lens. Place the negative carrier in the enlarger, switch on the enlarger light, open the aperture fully, and adjust the head so that the image is composed on the easel according to your requirements and is in focus. This is easier to do if the room lights are switched off. To substitute for the thickness of the printing paper, place a piece of white paper in the easel for this step.

Select the filtration and lens aperture as recommended by the paper manufacturer. With slide printing, there will also be a difference depending on which brand of original film you used; Kodachrome will need less cyan and a little less magenta than will Ektachrome. Under safelighting or in total darkness replace the blank paper in the easel with a sheet of unexposed printing paper, emulsion side up.

Make a series of test exposures at intervals of five seconds. Use a piece of dark card to cover all of the paper except for a strip. With each successive exposure, uncover another strip. This first test print can then be used, once processed, to determine the best exposure and filtration for the final print. When you come to make this final print, the basic steps are the same. Keep a note of the settings that give you the best result; this will save time and paper if you come to make another print of the same photograph.

COLOUR NEGATIVE PRINTS

Temperature and agitation are important when processing the paper – much more so than in black-and-white printing. This is one reason why drum processing is highly recommended. The alternative is to use trays, but their size makes it more difficult to maintain good temperature control. The example shown is of Ektacolor processed in Ektaprint chemicals. The recommended temperatures for all the solutions is 32.8°C (91°F), with a variation of no more than 0.3°C (0.5°F). You can work at lower temperatures, but this will affect the processing time, and it is better to be consistent so that you can repeat the processing sequence with confidence every time.

Some of the recently introduced processing kits allow you to make prints with chemicals at room

BELOW An example of a test print, from which to assess the best filtration and exposure for the final print. Refer to the section on black-and-white photography for the method of making a test print.

PRINT PROCESSING

1 Fill the print-loaded tube with warm water to bring the contents to the recommended temperature.

2 Discard the water and add pre-warmed developer, starting the timer.

3 Roll the tube by hand or on a motorized cradle to ensure even development.

4 Towards the end of the recommended time, discard so that the tube empties as the timer comes to a stop.

5 Add the bleach/fix, roll the tube as in 3, discard and refill with warm water.

6 Open the tube, pull the paper carefully out by its edge, and wash as recommended. Clean the tube.

7 When the wash is complete, gently sponge excess water off the print.

8 Hang the print to dry in a room that is free from dust. Drying can be accelerated with a hairdryer.

temperature – 20°C. This can make life easier since you will not need a tempering bath to maintain temperatures.

First prepare the solutions according to the instructions. With drum processing, there is a pre-wet step at the beginning to soften the paper emulsion and warm it up. This helps the developer to penetrate quickly and evenly, but it also means that the developer will have to be more concentrated than it would for tray processing. See the packed instructions.

Place the correct volume of each solution in a container, and place these containers in a deep warm water bath. Because the room temperature will be less than that of the processing solutions, they will cool gradually. Start with the water bath several degrees higher than the 32.8°C (91°F) needed. When the solutions reach the correct temperature, take the first and pour it into the drum (already loaded with a sheet of exposed paper).

Agitate the drum according to the drum manufacturer's recommendation. A motorized roller, although an extra expense, does this without any attention from the photographer, and is a great help. As with film processing, start the timer when all the solution is in the drum, and start to drain it away at the end so that the drum is emptied as the timer stops. Do not keep any of the used chemicals – throw them all away.

For the washing steps, either refill the drum each time, or remove the print and place it in an open tray, replacing the water every 30 seconds. In either case, continue to agitate. To dry, place the print on a smooth surface, image-side up, and remove all drops of water with a wide squeegee. Then, hang it from a clothes line by a clip attached to one corner, or place it on a clean towel, image-side up. A hair dryer will speed up the drying process.

OPPOSITE For convenience, and to avoid performing all steps in darkness, a print tube can be used for colour papers. This makes economical use of the more expensive colour chemicals, and is designed to be rotated through a bath of water thermostatically controlled at a constant temperature, known as a tempering bath.

BELOW AND LEFT More so than with black-and-white printing, temperature and agitation are important when processing colour paper. Your target when making a print depends upon personal taste – accuracy may be sacrificed for the sake of richer, deeper colours. Large format cameras which give 4×5in negatives will always produce a finer print, which is why professional photographers tend to use them whenever possible. As always for the amateur, there must be a trade-off between the relative improvement in quality and the greater expense of equipment.

127

COLOUR TRANSPARENCY PRINTS

Colour transparencies can be printed directly onto paper, using the same techniques described for colour negatives. The main difference is that, because a positive image is being made from another positive image, there are extra steps in the process, just as there are in processing colour slide film. Also, any changes to the filtration and exposure are the opposite of those for colour negative printing. When making a print directly from a slide, more light from the enlarger gives a lighter image and adding a filter of one colour gives an increase in the same colour to the printed image. The edges of the print, if they have been held down normally by the frame in the easel, appear black.

Most of the same equipment chosen for printing negatives can be used here. One difference is in the selection of printing filters, if you do not have a dial-in colour head on your enlarger. Cyan filters are often needed, so make sure that you have a selection of these, in different strengths. As with the negative printing process described earlier, a drum is recommended for ease and convenience. In fact, the need for absolute darkness when handling the paper also makes it safer.

The preparation and exposure stages are the same as for a colour negative, but filter and exposure changes are needed when you make corrections after the initial test print. Kodachrome slides, which are different in chemistry from other E-6 films, will need different filter packs when printing.

Mix and warm up the solutions. There are more of these than in negative printing, so make sure that the water bath is large enough for all the containers. Take the same precautions in maintaining the correct temperature: 37.8°C (100°F) with a variation of no more than 0.3°C (0.5°F). Follow the instructions step by step. As the print is hung up to dry, it will have a bluish cast, but this will clear during drying. Do not try to evaluate the print until it is quite dry.

■ CIBACHROME PRINTING

An alternative process for printing directly from colour slides is Cibachrome. This works on a quite different principle from reversal processing, and is, on the whole, simpler. The coloured dyes that make up the final image in the print are already present in the paper, and so are rich and long-lasting. There are just five steps in the processing,

including a water rinse after the development and a final water wash. The chemical kit is available in two litre and five litre packs; but as each sachet of chemical contains enough to make up a solution of exactly one litre, it is not necessary to make up the full amount. Do not, however, try to split up sachets. There are two paper types, one with a lustre finish the other with a gloss finish. Comprehensive instructions are provided with each kit.

CONTROLLING COLOUR RENDITION

By following the steps so far, you should be able to reach the point of having a print that is a close approximation to either the slide, or to what you consider the right treatment for the negative. There is, however, quite a bit more that can be done to control the final appearance of the print, and the techniques allow you considerable room for experiment. There is not the same degree of flexibility as in printing black-and-white photographs, but enough to be useful.

A high-contrast image is one of the classic problems in photography. The subject of the image is interesting, the view well-composed, but despite care in selecting the exposure when shooting, there is an insurmountable difference between the brightness of important parts of the scene. If the bright areas are rendered correctly, the shadows may be too dark, and conceal needed detail. Conversely, the right exposure of the shadows gives washed-out highlights. With colour printing there is, unfortunately, no choice of contrast grade in the paper, as there is for black-and-white. The answer is to give different exposure during the enlargement to different parts of the image.

There are two procedures: burning-in to give extra exposure to a selected area of the print; and dodging, to hold back the light from another area. In a complicated print, you may need to do both, in addition to a basic overall exposure for the rest of the image, but usually it is a matter of selecting one of the two techniques.

■ BURNING-IN

To do this, you will need to restrict the light from the enlarger head in the form of a hole, the shape of which should correspond with the area you want to affect. Either cut a hole in a sheet of black card and suspend this over the print, or cup your

LEFT AND BELOW Kodachrome has a very high blue sensitivity. In these pictures, the yellow cast from the setting sun (below) has been counteracted by the blue sensitivity of Kodachrome (left).

hands for a similar effect. It is important to move the hole around constantly, to prevent the edges of the extra exposure being too obvious on the print. When printing a negative, this technique will darken an area; when printing a slide, it will lighten an area.

DODGING

In dodging, you block the light reaching an area. With a negative, this lightens the area; with a slide, it darkens it. The tools are shapes cut from black card stuck onto the ends of wire (proprietary tools are also available). For larger areas, you can use your hand, bunched into the appropriate shape. See section on printing black-and-white.

LOCAL COLOUR CONTROL

Once you have mastered the skills of dodging and burning-in, try a similar procedure with colour. The colour ring-around shown on page 119 may indicate that a selected area of the print could do with a slight colour change; for instance, you might want to increase the warmth of an evening sky. To do this, use a filter in the same way that you would use a dodging tool. When printing a negative, use the complementary colour to the one you want to introduce in the image; with a slide, use the same colour of filter.

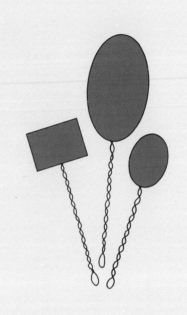

PRINTING: ASSESSING THE RESULTS

Particularly when you start printing, it is unlikely that you will get both the exposure and filtration right first time. Colour is, in any case, a subjective variable, and at the printing stage you may decide to alter the balance. Judging the results after printing a slide is easier than from a negative, as the original slide is at hand for direct comparison. A negative, on the other hand, can only be judged properly for colour once it has been printed, so that there is no absolute reference standard. In either case, it is a good idea to tackle the assessment in two stages. First, judge the exposure, then the colour balance.

The test print will give you a series of exposures to choose from. Keep a note on the back of the test print of the enlarger settings; if you followed the recommendations given earlier, the shortest exposure will have been five seconds and for each adjacent strip an additional five seconds. Remember

For a smaller area, a dodging tool is used. This can be shaped to fit the exact area to be dodged. Hold it well above the print to cast an out-of-focus shadow and keep it moving.

Moving your hand continuously will give a soft edge to the shading.

This table shows filter factors from which you can calculate your new exposure to allow for filter changes – divide your original time by the factor(s) for the filter(s) you have removed. Then multiply the result by the factor(s) for each filter you have added and round off your result to the nearest second.

Filter	Factor	Filter	Factor	Filter	Factor	Filter	Factor	Filter	Factor	Filter	Factor
05Y	1.1	05M	1.2	05C	1.1	05R	1.2	05G	1.1	05B	1.1
10Y	1.1	10M	1.3	10C	1.2	10R	1.3	10G	1.2	10B	1.3
20Y	1.1	20M	1.5	20C	1.3	20R	1.5	20G	1.3	20B	1.6
30Y	1.1	30M	1.7	30C	1.4	30R	1.7	30G	1.4	30B	2.0
40Y	1.1	40M	1.9	40C	1.5	40R	1.9	40G	1.5	40B	2.4
50Y	1.1	50M	2.1	50C	1.6	50R	2.2	50G	1.7	50B	2.9

that extra exposure, when printing from a negative, gives a darker image, while extra exposure with a slide results in a paler print. Look for clean highlights and rich, dark shadow areas, with the majority of tones in a typical scene having average density.

Next assess the colour balance. With experience, it is fairly easy to see in which direction the image has drifted away from neutral, but it helps at the start to have a reference.

It does not matter that the images are different; look for the same degree of colour imbalance and read the filter recommendation alongside. As you can see, negatives and slides need opposite filtration adjustment.

An alternative method is to use one of several proprietary kits for finding the best filtration. One useful tip for when you start printing for the first time, with an unfamiliar enlarger and paper, is to take a photograph that contains the two easiest colours to judge – neutral grey and average skin tones. We are so familiar with these that our eyes can discriminate colour shifts without difficulty. An 18% grey card (used for reflected exposure metering) is ideal. The prints can then be compared next to this.

MAKING A FILTRATION TEST

Use the exposure test as a basis for estimating the likely filtration. Accurate estimation at this stage comes with experience, but at the start you may find it easier to try a few different filtrations (right). Do not make the changes too great, and remember to compensate in exposure for filtration changes. Make three or four exposures with different filter combinations.

Red bias

Green bias

Correctly balanced

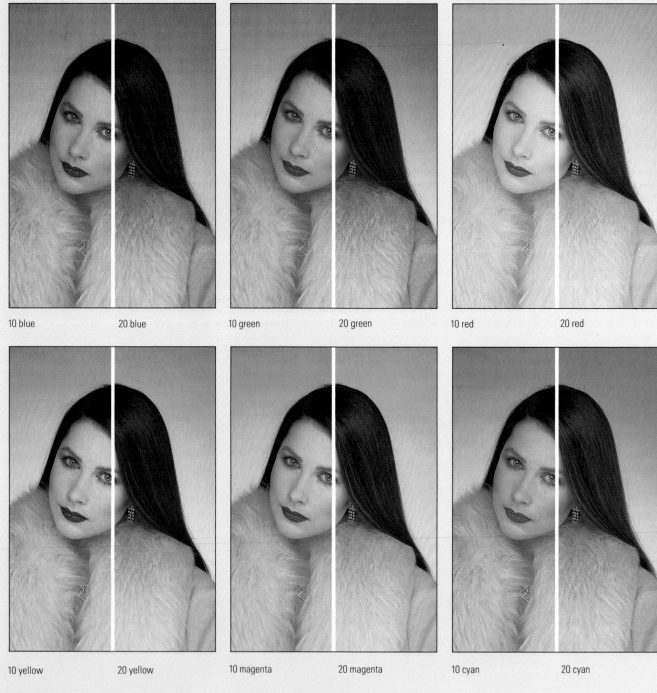

10 blue | 20 blue | 10 green | 20 green | 10 red | 20 red

10 yellow | 20 yellow | 10 magenta | 20 magenta | 10 cyan | 20 cyan

These strips of different colour filtrations show the effects of using varying strengths of the primary and complementary filters. Many printers make their own customized colour cast identification chart called a ringaround. This is a series of prints made at different, known filtrations from a very well exposed negative. To make your own, start with a 'perfect' print from the chosen negative, then make a series of prints, changing the filtration in units of ten up to 30 or 40 units in each of the filter colours. Mark the prints for reference.

CARING FOR PHOTOGRAPHS

8

MOUNTING PRINTS

With the final enlargement made, and spotted or retouched as necessary, you can begin to think of how to display it to best advantage. While one alternative is to leave prints loose in a box or folder, this is little protection against handling. For your best prints, consider an album or mount.

In a photographic album, the paper and board should be of archival materials (some papers, and most adhesives, give off volatile compounds that will, in time, cause the image to fade and discolour). For this same reason, avoid sticking prints to paper with glue or double-sided adhesive tape. Instead, use either an album in which the pages have glassine covers that hold prints in place, or use paper corner mounts.

For a more prominent display, however, a print needs to be mounted on board. There is a special technique for this, using dry mounting tissue (this is archivally sound) and some kind of heated press. A proper press is ideal, but is also an additional expense; if you do not think its cost is justified by the number of prints you intend to mount, it is possible to make do with an ordinary household iron.

■ EQUIPMENT AND MATERIALS

You will need: a packet of dry mounting tissue or a photographically inert cement (Kodak, for instance, make both); mounting board, also photographically inert; a dry mounting press and tacking iron, or else a household iron set to the lowest level for a synthetic fabric; a rotary print cutter, or a sharp

MOUNTING A PRINT

1 Measure the picture area that is to appear when mounted, and mark the frame lines on the borders of the print in pencil.

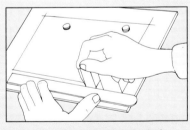

2 Mark these dimensions on the back of a sheet of thick card, and, using an angled mat cutter cut each of the lines up to the corners. Trim with a scalpel.

3 On a second sheet of card – the backing for the mount – position the print and mark round the corners in pencil.

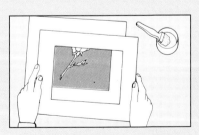

4 Having sprayed or brushed a light, even covering of glue onto the back of the print, roll it down onto the backing card using a sheet of tracing paper to avoid making marks.

5 Apply glue to the edges of the backing card, position the top piece of card, and press down firmly.

6 The mounted print is ready for display, but handle it carefully until the glue is completely dry.

133

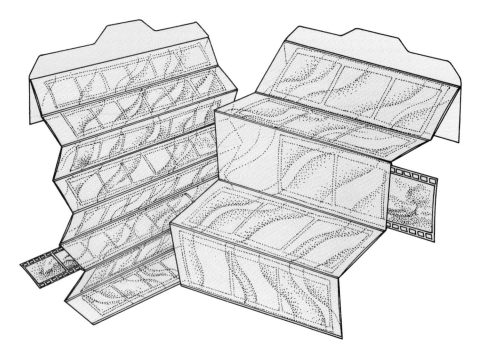

LEFT Fortunately for the photographer, many processing labs return negatives in purpose-built folders. These are available for both 35mm (right) and 120 (far right) format films.

blade (a craft-knife or a scalpel) used with a metal straight-edge and setsquare. For making overlay frames, a mat cutter is ideal, as this can be set to make an angled cut. Thin cotton gloves protect the print's surface from finger grease.

■ COLD MOUNTING

Use only an adhesive that has been made specifically for mounting photographs, or it will make the image deteriorate in time. There are no special procedures, but it is usually necessary to press the print and mounting board flat under some heavy books after the adhesive has been applied.

FILING NEGATIVES

Unlike slides, which are themselves the finished product, negatives are a working stage in black-and-white photography, and need a different storage system. The images they carry do not need to be immediately easy to see, but they do need to be stored safely, and in such a way that they can be taken out and used in an enlarger rapidly. They also need a separate visual reference system – that is, accessible files of contact sheets.

A normal negative carrier in an enlarger accepts short strips of film, and this is the way negatives should be cut and filed. Avoid cutting individual frames from a roll as much as possible: a single negative is more difficult to handle, and so more likely to slip from your fingers; it will also sit less securely in most negative carriers. The usual way of cutting a roll of 36 35mm exposures is into six strips of six frames each. 6×6cm negatives from a 120 roll will normally cut evenly into strips of three or four.

Standard negative envelopes are translucent, although transparent slips are easier for identification. In either case, the most widely used filing system is in sheets divided into sufficient strips to hold one roll of film.

Flicking through negative files in search of a particular picture is tedious and inefficient, hence the need for a full set of contact sheets. Having made the contact sheet the next step is to relate negative sheets to contact sheets, for which you will need some labelling or numbering system. One of the most straightforward methods is simply by the order in which you shot the rolls: give the same number to the negative sheet and to the contact sheet for easy reference.

With a normal print, you should never write on the back in ink – the pressure of the pen may go through and emboss the emulsion, and the ink may eventually cause a stain. This is not the case with a contact sheet, however, and you can make an exception; use the back to write down all the essential details, such as the date, place, subject, type of film and any special procedures, such as push-processing. You might also want to include a few notes on the printing. The sheet can then be stored loose, in a box or folder, or in a ring-bound book file; negative sheets and contact sheets can be kept together or separately.

GLOSSARY

A

Aberration Lens fault in which light rays are not focused properly, thereby degrading the image. It includes chromatic and spherical aberration, coma, astigmatism and field curvature.

Achromatic lens A lens constructed of different types of glass, to reduce chromatic aberration. The simplest combination is of two elements, one of flint glass, the other of crown glass.

Acutance The objective measurement of how well an edge is recorded in a photographic image.

Aerial Perspective The impression of depth in a scene that is conveyed by haze.

Additive process The process of combining lights of different colours. A set of three primary colours combined equally produces white.

Anastigmat A compound lens, using different elements to reduce optical aberrations.

Angle of view Angle of the scene included across the picture frame by a particular lens. This varies with the focal length of the lens and the film format.

Aperture In most lenses, the aperture is an adjustable circular opening centred on the lens axis. It is the part of the lens that admits light.

Aperture-priority Automatic camera mode in which the photographer selects the aperture manually; the appropriate shutter speed is then set automatically according to the information from the camera's metering system.

Area light Photographic lamp/s enclosed in a box-like structure, the front of which is covered with a diffusing material such as opalescent plastic. Light is diffused by increasing the area of the light source. Also known as soft light, window light or 'fish-fryer'.

Auto focus System in which the focus is adjusted automatically, either passively by measuring the contrast of edges, or actively by measuring the reflection of an ultrasonic pulse.

Automatic exposure control Camera system where the photo-electric cell that measures the light reaching the film plane is linked to the shutter or lens aperture, adjusting exposure automatically.

B

Background roll A standard type of studio background, in the form of heavy-gauge coloured paper, in 9ft (3m) wide rolls.

Barn doors Adjustable flaps that fit at the front of a photographic studio lamp to prevent light from spilling at the sides. Normally two or four hinged flaps on a frame.

Base The support material for an emulsion – normally plastic or paper.

Base density The minimum density of the film base in a transparency or negative. Determines the maximum brightness of highlights in a transparency.

Base lighting Lighting directed upwards from beneath a subject. Also known as ground lighting.

Boom Counter-weighted lighting support in the form of a metal arm that pivots on a vertical stand. Useful for suspending lights high over a subject.

Bounce flash Diffusion of the light from a flash unit, by directing it towards a reflective surface, such as a ceiling or wall. This scatters the light rays, giving a softer illumination.

Bounce light Diffusion of any light source in the same way as described for bounce flash.

Bracketing A method of compensating for uncertainties in exposure, by making a series of exposures of a single subject, each varying by a progressive amount from the estimated correct aperture/speed setting.

Brightness range The range of tones in a photographic subject, from darkest to lightest. Usually measured as a ratio or in f-stops.

C

Capacitor Electrical device that allows a charge to be built up and stored. An integral part of electronic flash units.

Cartridge camera/film Photographic system in which the film is enclosed in a plastic cartridge, simplifying loading and unloading. Designed for amateur use.

CdS cell Cadmium sulphide cell used commonly in through-the-lens light meters. Its proportionate resistance to the quantity of light received is the basis of exposure measurement.

Central processing unit (CPU) In an automatic camera, the part of the electronic circuitry that co-ordinates the programming.

Centre-weighted exposure Standard method of exposure measurement in TTL-metering cameras in which extra value is given to the tones in the centre of the picture.

Characteristic curve Curve plotted on a graph from two axes – exposure and density – used to describe the characteristics and performance of sensitive emulsions.

Chromogenic film Photographic emulsion in which dyes are formed at the sites of the silver grains. Normal for colour film.

Circle of confusion The disc of light formed by an imaginary lens. When small enough, it appears to the eye as a point, and at this size the image appears sharp.

Click stop The graduation of the aperture ring on a lens allows the change between individual f-stops to be felt and heard.

Clip test A short strip from an exposed film that is processed in advance to determine whether any adjustment is needed in processing. Useful when the exposure conditions are uncertain.

Coating A thin deposited surface on a lens, to reduce flare by intererence of light waves.

Colour balance Adjustment made at any stage of photography from film manufacturers to post-production, to ensure that neutral greys in the subject appear neutral in the photograph.

Colour cast An overall bias in a photograph towards one particular colour.

Colour compensating filter Filter used to alter the colour of light. Available in primary and complementary colours at different strengths and used to correct deficiences in the lighting and film manufacture.

Colour conversion filter Coloured filter that alters the colour temperature of light.

Colour temperature The temperature to which an inert substance would have to be heated in order for it to glow at a particular colour. The scale of colour temperature significant for photography ranges from the reddish colours of approximately 2000°K through standard 'white' at 5400°K, to the bluish colours above 6000°K.

Complementary colours A pair of colours that, when combined together in equal proportions, produce white light (additive process).

Condenser Simple lens system that concentrates light into a beam. Often used in enlargers.

Contact sheet A print of all the frames of a roll of film arranged in strips, same-size, from which negatives can be selected for enlargement.

Contrast Difference in brightness between adjacent areas of tone. In photographic emulsions, it is also the rate of increase in density measured against exposure.

Contrast range The range of tones, from dark to light, of which film or paper is capable of recording. Usually measured as a ratio or in f-stops.

Cyan Blue-green, complementary to red. Produces white in combination with magenta and yellow by the additive process.

D

Daylight film Colour film balanced for exposure by daylight or some other source with a colour temperature of 5400°K, such as electronic flash.

Dedicated flash The integration of a flash unit with the camera's automatic exposure system.

Definition The subjective effect of graininess and sharpness combined.

Density In photographic emulsions, the ability of a developed silver deposit to block transmitted light.

Depth of field The distance through which the subject may extend and still form an acceptably sharp image, in front of and beyond the place of critical focus, Depth of field can be increased by stopping the lens down to a smaller aperture. It is a subjective measurement.

Depth of focus The distance through which the film plane can be moved and still record an acceptably sharp image.

Diaphragm An adjustable opening that controls the amount of light passing through a lens. Often referred to as the aperture diaphragm.

Diffraction The scattering of light waves when they strike the edge of an opaque surface.

Diffuser Material that scatters transmitted light and increases the area of the light source.

DIN Logarithmically progressive rating of the sensitivity of a film to light (Deutsche Industrie Norm). Currently being replaced by the ISO rating.

Direct reading Common term for reflecting light reading.

Disc camera/film Amateur photographic system in which the film frames are arranged on a flat disc.

Documentary photography Type of photography in which an accurate, objective record, undistorted by interpretation, is held to be the ideal.

Dye-sensitization The standard manufacturing process of adding dyes to emulsion in order to control its spectral sensitivity. Used in the manufacture of normal black-and-white films to make them panchromatic.

E

Effects light A photographic light used to produce a distinct visual effect rather than to provide basic illumination. A spotlight to give a halo effect to hair in a portrait is one example.

Electronic flash Artificial light source produced by passing a charge across two electrodes in a gas. The colour balance is about 5400°K.

Emulsion Light-sensitive substance composed of halides suspended in gelatin, used for photographic film and paper.

Exposure In photography, the amount of light reaching an emulsion, being the product of intensity and time.

Exposure latitude For film, the increase in exposure that can be made from the minimum necessary to record shadow detail, while still presenting highlight detail.

Exposure value (EV) Notation of exposure settings for cameras that links aperture and shutter speed. A single EV number can, for example, represent 1/125 at f5.6 and 1/500 at f2.8.

F

F-number The notation for relative aperture, which is the ratio of the focal length to the diameter of the aperture. The light-gathering power of lenses is usually described by the widest f-stop of which they are capable, and lens aperture rings are normally calibrated in a standard series: f1, f1.4, f2, f2.8, f4, f5.6, f8, f11, f16, f22, f32 and so on, each of these stops differing from its adjacent stop by a factor of 2.

Field camera Traditional folding design of view camera, often of mahogany construction with a flat-bed base, that is sufficiently portable for carrying on location.

Fill The illumination of shadow areas in a scene.

Fill-flash As fill (above) but performed with an electronic flash, usually camera-mounted.

Film plane In a camera, the plane at the back in which the film lies and on which the focus is set.

Film speed rating The sensitivity of film to

light, measured on a standard scale, now normally ISO, formerly either ASA or DIN.

Filter factor The number by which the exposure must be multiplied in order to compensate for the loss of light due to absorption by a filter.

Fish-eye lens A very wide-angle lens.

Flag A matt black sheet held in position between a lamp and the camera lens to reduce flare.

Flare Non-image-forming light, caused by scattering and reflection, that degrades the quality of an image. Coating is used to reduce it.

Flash See *Electronic flash.*

Flash guide number Notation used to determine the aperture setting when using electronic flash. It is proportionate to the output of the flash unit.

Flash synchronization Camera system that ensures that the peak light output from a flash unit coincides with the time that the shutter is fully open.

Focal length The distance between the centre of a lens (the principal point) and its focal point.

Focal plane The plane at which a lens forms a sharp image.

Focal plane shutter Shutter located close to the focal plane using two blinds that form an adjustable gap which moves across the film area. The size of the gap determines the exposure.

Focal point The point on either side of a lens where light rays entering parallel to the axis converge.

Focus The point at which light rays are converged by a lens.

Fresnel screen A viewing screen that incorporates a Fresnel lens. This has a stepped convex surface that performs the same function as a condenser lens, distributing image brightness over the entire area of the screen, but is much thinner.

G

Gel Common term for coloured filter sheeting, normally used over photographic lamps.

Grade Classification of photographic printing paper by contrast. Grades 0 to 4 are the most common, although they are not precisely comparable across makes.

Grain An individual light-sensitive crystal, normally of silver bromide.

Graininess The subjective impression when viewing a photograph of granularity under normal viewing conditions. The eye cannot resolve individual grains, only overlapping clusters.

Granularity The measurement of the size and distribution of grains in an emulsion.

Ground-glass screen Sheet of glass finely ground to a translucent finish on one side, used to make image focusing easier when viewing.

H

Half-tone An image that appears at normal viewing distance to have continuous gradation of tones, but which is made up of a fine pattern of dots of solid ink or colours.

Hardener Chemical agent – commonly chrome or potassium alum – that combines with the gelatin of a film to make it more resistant to scratching.

Hyperfocal distance The closest distance at which a lens records a subject sharply when focused at infinity. It varies with the aperture.

I

Incident light reading Exposure measurement of the light source that illuminates the subject. It is therefore independent of the subject's own characteristics.

Infra-red radiation Electromagnetic radiation from 730 nanometers to $1/32$in (1mm), longer in wavelength than light. It is emitted by hot bodies.

Instant film Photographic system pioneered by the Polaroid corporation, in which processing is initiated as soon as the exposed film is withdrawn from the camera and is normally completed within a minute or so.

Instant-return mirror The angled viewing mirror in a SLR camera, which flips up to allow the film to be exposed and then immediately returns.

Integral masking The addition of dyes to colour negative film in its manufacture to compensate for deficiencies in the image forming dyes.

Internegative A negative copy of transparency Intergative film is formulated to prevent any build-up of contrast.

ISO (International Standard Organization) Film speed notation to replace the ASA and DIN systems, made up of a combination of these two.

J

Joule Unit of electronic flash output, equal to one watt-second. The power of different units can be compared with this measurement.

K

Kelvin (K) The standard unit of thermodynamic temperature, calculated by adding 273 to degrees centrigrade/Celsius. In photography it is a measure of colour temperature.

Key light The main light source.

Key tone The most important tone is a scene being photographed that must be rendered accurately.

L

Latitude The variation in exposure that an emulsion can tolerate and still give an acceptable image. Usually measured in f-stops.

LCD (Liquid crystal diode) A solid-state display system used in viewfinder information displays particularly. Consumes less power than LEDs (light emitting diodes).

Lens A transparent device for converging or diverging rays of light by refraction. Convex lenses are thicker at the centre than at the edges; concave lenses are thicker at the edges than at the centre.

Lens flare Non-image-forming light reflected from lens surfaces that degrades the quality of the image.

Lens hood Lens attachment that shades the front element from non-image-forming light that can cause flare.

Lens speed Common lens designation in terms of maximum light-gathering power. The figure used is the maximum aperture.

Long-focus lens Lens with a focal length longer than the diagonal of the film format. For 35mm film, anything longer than about 50mm is therefore long-focus, although in practice the term is usually applied to lenses with at least twice the standard focal length.

M

Macro Abbreviation for photomacrographic, applied to close-up photography of at least life-size reproduction. In particular, used to designate lenses and other equipment used for this purpose.

Macrophotography The photography of large-scale objects. Hardly ever used to mean this, but often misused to mean 'photomacrography'.

Magnification Size relationship between image and its subject, expressed as a multiple of the dimension of the subject.

Manual operation The operation of camera, flash or other equipment in non-automatic modes.

Masking Blocking specific areas of an emulsion from light. For example, a weak positive image, when combined with the negative, can be used to mask the highlights so as to produce a less contrasty print.

Mercury vapour lamp Form of lighting sometimes encountered in available light photography. It has a discontinous spectrum and reproduces as blue-green on colour film.

Mired value A measurement of colour temperature that facilitates the comparison of different light sources. It is calculated by dividing 1,000,000 by the colour temperature of the light source in Kelvins.

Mirror lens Compound lens that forms an image by reflection from curved mirrors rather than by refraction through lenses. By folding the light paths, its length is much shorter that that of traditional lenses of the same focal length.

Mode In camera technology, the form in which the basic functions (including exposure measurement, aperture and shutter speed settings) are operated. Many automatic cameras have a choice of modes, from a high degree of automation to manual operation.

Modelling lamp A continuous-light lamp fitted next to the flashtube in studio flash units that is used to show what the lighting effect will be when the discharge is triggered. Modelling lamps are usually low-wattage and either tungsten or fluorescent and do not interfere with the actual exposure.

Monopod Single leg of a tripod, as a lightweight camera support for hand-held shooting.

Motor drive Device that either attaches to a camera or is built into it, that motorizes the film transport, enabling a rapid sequence of photographs.

Multiple exposure Method of combining more than one image on a single frame of film by making successive exposures of different subjects.

Multiple flash The repeated triggering of a flash unit to increase exposure (with a static subject).

Multi-pattern metering The metering system in which areas of the image frame are measured separately, and weighted according to a predetermined programme.

N

Negative Photographic image with reversed tones (and reversed colours if colour film) used to make a positive image, normally a print by projection.

Neutral density Density that is equal across all visible wavelengths, resulting in absence of colour.

137

O

Opalescent Milky or cloudy white, translucent quality of certain materials, valuable in the even diffusion of a light source.

Optical axis Line passing through the centre of a lens system. A light ray following this line would not be bent.

Optimum aperture The aperture setting at which the highest quality images are formed by a lens. Often two or three f-stops less than maximum.

OTF metering Off-the-film metering – a TTL system in which the exposure is measured from the image that is projected inside the camera at the film plane.

P

Panchromatic film Film that is sensitive to all the colours of the visible spectrum.

Panning Smooth rotation of the camera so as to keep a moving subject continuously in frame.

Parallax The apparent movement of two objects relative to each other when viewed from different positions.

Penataprism Five-sided prism, which rectifies the image left-to-right and top-to-bottom.

Perspective correction (PC) lens A lens with covering power greater than the film area, part of which can be shifted to bring different parts of the image into view. Mainly used to correct converging verticals in architectural photography.

Photo-electric cell Light sensitive cell used to measure exposure. Some cells produce electricity when exposed to light; other react to light by offering an electrical resistance.

Photomacrography Close-up photography with magnifications in the range of about $1\times$ to $10\times$.

Plane of sharp focus The plane at which an image is sharply focused by a lens. In a fixed-body camera it is normally vertical and perpendicular to the lens axis, but it can be tilted by means of camera movements.

Polarization Restriction of the direction of vibration of light. Normal light vibrates at right angles to its direction of travel in every plane; a plane-polarizing filter (the most common in photography) restricts this vibration to one plane only. There are several applications, the most usual being to eliminate reflections from water and non-metal surfaces.

Post-production The photographic processes that take place after the image has been developed including re-touching, special effects and treatment.

Printing controls Shading and printing-in techniques used during englargement to lighten or darken certain parts of a photographic print.

Printing-in Printing technique of selectively increasing exposure over certain areas of the image.

Prism Transparent substances shaped so as to refract light in a controlled manner.

Programmed shutter Electronically operated shutter with variable speeds that is linked to the camera's TTL meter. When a particular aperture setting is selected, the shutter speed is automatically adjusted to give a standard exposure.

Pull-processing Giving film less development than normal, in order to compensate for overexposure or to reduce contrast.

Push-processing Giving film more development than normal, in order to compensate for underexposure or to increase contrast.

R

Rangefinder Arrangement of mirror, lens and prism that measures distance by means of a binocular system. Used on direct viewfinder cameras for accurate focusing.

Reciprocity failure (reciprocity effect) At very short and very long exposures, the reciprocity law ceases to hold true, and an extra exposure is needed. With colour film, the three dye layers suffer differently, causing a colour cast. Reciprocity failure differs from emulsion to emulsion.

Reciprocity law EXPOSURE – INTENSITY $\times$ TIME. In other words, the amount of exposure that the film receives in a camera is a product of the size of the lens aperture (intensity) and the shutter speed (time).

Reflected light reading Exposure measurement of the light reflected from the subject (cf *Incident light reading*). Through-the-lens meters use this method, and is well-suited to subjects of average reflectance.

Reflector Surface used to reflect light.

Reproduction ratio The relative proportions of the size of the subject and its range.

Resolution The ability of a lens to distinguish between closely spaced objects, also known as resolving power.

Reticulation Crazed effect on a film emulsion caused by subjecting the softened gelatin to extremes of temperature change.

Reversal film Photographic emulsion which, when developed, gives a positive image (commonly called a transparency). So called because of one stage in the development when the film is briefly re-exposed either chemically or to light, thus reversing the image which would otherwise be negative.

Ringflash Electronic flash in the shape of a ring, used in front of and surrounding the camera lens. The effect is of virtually shadowless lighting.

Rollfilm Film rolled on a spool with a dark paper backing. The most common current rollfilm format is 120.

S

Safelight Light source used in a darkroom with a colour and intensity that does not affect the light-sensitive materials for which it is designed.

Sandwich Simple, physical combination of two sheets of film: transparencies for projection, negatives for printing.

Scoop Smoothly curving studio background, used principally to eliminate the horizon line.

Selenium cell Photo-electric cell which generates its own electricity in proportion to incident light.

Shading Photographic printing technique where light is held back from selected parts of the image.

Shadow detail The darkest visible detail in a subject or in the positive image often sets the lower limit for exposure.

Sharpness The subjective impression of acutance when viewing a photograph.

Shift lens See *Perspective control lens*.

Short-focus lens Lens with a focal length shorter than the diagonal of the film format. For the 35mm format, short-focus lenses generally range shorter than 35mm.

Shutter Camera mechanism that controls the period of time that image-focusing light is allowed to fall on the film.

Shutter priority Automatic camera mode in which the photographer selects the shutter speed manually; the appropriate aperture is then set automatically according to the information from the camera's metering system.

Single lens reflex (SLR) Camera design that allows the image focused on the film plane to be previewed. A hinged mirror that diverts the light path is the basis of the system.

SLR See *Single lens reflex*.

Slave unit Device that responds to the light emission from one flash unit to activate additional flash units simultaneously.

Snoot Generally, cylindrical fitting for a light source, used to throw a circle of light.

Soft-focus filter A glass filter with an irregular or etched surface that reduces image sharpness and increases flare in a controlled fashion. Normally used for a flattening effect in portraiture.

Spotlight A lamp containing a focusing system that concentrates a narrow beam of light in a controllable way.

Spotmeter Hand-held exposure meter of great accuracy, measuring reflected light over a small, precise angle of view.

Standard lens See *Normal lens.*

Step wedge Strip of developed film containing a measured graduated scale of density. Used for exposing alongside separation negatives to check accuracy of exposure.

Stills video Electronic camera which records a still image on floppy video disc or ram card.

Stop bath Chemical that neutralizes the action of the developer on an emulsion, effectively stopping development.

Strobe Abbreviation for 'stroboscopic light'. A rapidly repeating flash unit, used for multiple-exposure photographs of moving subjects.

Substantive film Colour film in which the colour-forming dyes are included at manufacture. Most colour films are of this type.

Substitute reading Exposure measurement of a surface or subject that is similar in tone or appearance to the subject about to be photographed.

T

Tele-converter Supplementary lens that attaches between a telephoto lens and the camera body to increase the focal length.

Telephoto lens Design of long-focus lens in which the length of the lens is less than the focal length

Test strip Test of various exposures made with an enlarger.

Through-the-lens (TTL) meter Exposure meter built into the camera, normally located close to the instant-return mirror of a single lens reflex or to the pentaprism.

Time exposure Exposure of several seconds or more that must be timed by the photographer.

Toner Chemicals that add an overall colour to a processed black-and-white image, by means of bleaching and dyeing.

Tungsten-balance film Film manufactured for use with tungsten lighting without the need for balancing filters. Type A film is balanced for 3400°K; the more common type B film is balanced for 3200°K.

Tungsten lighting Artificial lighting caused by heating a filament of tungsten to a temperature where it emits light.

U

Ultraviolet radiation Although it is invisible, most films are sensitive to this electromagnetic radiation.

V

Variable contrast paper Printing paper with a single emulsion which can be used at different degrees of contrast by means of selected filters.

W

Wavelength of light The distance between peaks in a wave of light. This distance, among other things, determines the colour.

Wetting agent Chemical that weakens the surface tension of water, and so reduces the risk of drying marks on film.

Wide-angle lens Lens with an angle of view wider than that of the human eye and having a short focal length.

Z

Zoom lens Lens with a continuously variable focal length over a certain range at any given focus and aperture. It is generated by differential movement of the lens elements.

INDEX

ACKNOWLEDGEMENTS

All photographs taken by Michael Freeman with the exception of the following: p7 Gavin Hodge, p9 below E.T. Archive, pp31 and 71 top right David Kilpatrick, p69 Peter Conrad.

The publishers would like to thank the following for providing information and equipment for photography: Durst Phototechnik; Jessop of Leicester Ltd; Minolta (UK) Ltd; Mosta Posta, London; Olympus Optical Co. Ltd; Pentax (UK) Ltd; Polaroid (UK) Ltd.